Turkey: Thwarted Ambition

1.
Introduction

At the end of the Cold War every country was forced to re-examine the fundamental assumptions that had formed their security policies for the last 45 years. Among the "victors" of the Cold War, few countries were faced with a more disparate set of new circumstances than Turkey. Unlike the United States and Western Europe, "victory" for Turkey had a very ambivalent quality. Almost overnight Turkey moved from being the buttressing flank of one strategic region, to the epicenter of a new one.

In a bipolar world Turkey had had the luxury of an uncomplicated security policy in which, broadly speaking, it aligned with the West, opposed the Soviet Union, and ignored the rest. In the new security environment, Turkey's geographical position and its military strength now made it a European, Balkan, Middle Eastern, Near Eastern, Caucasian, Mediterranean, Aegean, and Black Sea power. Sharing borders with Greece, Bulgaria, Georgia, Armenia, Iran, Iraq, and Syria, Turkey's control of the Bosphorus Straits and the Dardenelles also made it a Black Sea neighbor of Russia, the Ukraine, Romania and Moldova. Turkey's ethnic roots lay in Central Asia, the Caucasus, and the Balkans, influencing its interests, concerns, and sympathies. Its Muslim identity demanded a

1

community of interest in the Middle East, through Pakistan, and across to South East Asia. This span of responsibility was a source of both excitement and concern, but these emotions were not often shared by its allies.

Turkey was an active participant in the Gulf War, and in its wake President Turgut Ozal stated, "It is my conviction that Turkey should leave its former passive and hesitant policies and engage in an active foreign policy."[1] Between 1991 and 1993, Turkey seemed to embrace Ozal's vision, embarking on a broad range of diplomatic activity in Central Asia, the Trans-Caucasus, the Middle East, and the Black Sea area. These ambitions were supported by a wide range of Turkish public opinion, and by many observers in the West,[2] particularly in the United States.[3] None of the immediate and demanding post-Cold War issues of Bosnia, the Middle East Peace Process, Iraqi sanctions, Operation *Provide Comfort*, Trans-Caucasus separatism, Russian activities in the "Near Abroad," CFE flank issues, NATO enlargement, Cyprus, Central Asia, and energy pipelines could be discussed without reference to Turkey. Enthusiasm and concern colored assessments of how Turkey would address these new challenges and opportunities. Many of these assessments were flawed by poor understanding of the dynamics of the Turkish state, society, and economy, or by lack of knowledge about the consistent elements in Turkish foreign policy.

In his history of the First World War, Churchill wrote, "I can recall no great sphere of policy about which the British Government was less completely informed than the Turkish."[4] He wrote this in 1929, some 6 years after the Treaty of Lausanne had formally recognized the new Republic of Turkey. Written with the benefit of hindsight, his comments encompassed not only the causes and consequences of the disastrous Gallipoli campaign, but the whole conduct of British policy toward the late Ottoman Empire and the foundations of modern Turkey. The British were not alone in misunderstanding Turkey. Throughout the West, lack of comprehension was compounded by historical antipathy, while political and intellectual objectivity was distorted through the cloud of religious antagonism and cultural contempt.

This attitude persisted, and it was reflected in bland assumptions by the West regarding President Ozal's decision to close the Iraqi oil pipeline, only 4 days after the invasion of Kuwait. To many it seemed the natural response of a NATO ally to U.S. calls for assistance. In fact the active response of the Turkish Government was one of the most significant watersheds in Turkish security policy since the decisions to enter the Korean War and to join NATO. While Ozal's decision, in both style and substance, created bitter divisions in the Turkish political elite, it was barely noticed in the West, but did reflect the particular nature of Turkish state and society.

Geopolitics is "the relation of international political power to the geographical setting."[5] While geography itself does not determine specific political behavior, it nonetheless defines territory, resources, and neighbors, and thereby conditions, shapes, and influences a country's security policy choices. Historically, any ruler of Anatolia has to be a Janus, looking both East and West, and thereby drawn into the affairs of significantly different areas of political and cultural influence. It is this feature that makes Turkey *sui generis* and therefore such a difficult country to classify. Hence, while Mustafa Kemal (hereafter called Ataturk)[6] espoused a nationalist, secular, Western-oriented destiny, Turkey's position and the nature of its society could never make this an uncontested decision.

However, these choices were accepted as "national policy" in Turkey until well into the Cold War and were rarely challenged or criticized. Ataturk had entrusted this "national mission" to elites in the military and civil service establishment, and security policy was seen as a state monopoly over which politics and public opinion had little influence. Much of this acceptance was based on success. In over 70 years of existence as a state, Turkey survived the desperate circumstances of its foundation, the enduring antagonism or antipathy of most of its neighbors, the cataclysm of the Second World War, periodic Middle East conflict, and the global confrontation of the Cold War. Through all this the Republic was never invaded, defeated, or occupied, nor did it concede an inch of Turkish soil. In addition, the material benefits were clear.

This success was based on a firm set of security priorities, a hard-headed assessment of the realistic limits and potential of Turkish power, and the ability of the state to pursue this policy single mindedly. The Turkish state inherited from the Ottomans an ability to distinguish between "permanent" policy, taken as the foundation of all its actions and activities, and "temporary" policy, followed for a period in accordance with the circumstances.[7] The consistent policy aspects were not always discerned by those watching events in Turkey, and attention was more often captured by the military interventions, the often fractured state of Turkish politics, or by Turco-Greek confrontation, particularly over Cyprus. Therefore the full significance of Ozal's statement in March 1991 was missed.

From the 1950s to the 1990s, Turkey underwent major socioeconomic change. This domestic dynamism led to debate over the Western orientation of security policy, but control of security policy by the elite ensured that it remained consistent with Ataturk's aspirations. However, the end of the Cold War, the removal of a direct Russian threat, ambivalence over the Gulf War, and the opening of new horizons exacerbated divisions. As the implications of the New World Order became clearer, so time and again Turkish opinion perceived Western foreign policy priorities running counter to its interests. Where these interests and priorities coincided, Turkey often found its ambitions thwarted by its geographical position or economic potential. What it felt to be a geostrategic position of continuing or growing importance, others now saw as one of potential liability. In an era of reduced threat, critics of Turkey had the luxury to question its political culture, the nature of its democracy, and its human rights record. Internal problems carried into the foreign policy arena, and external opinion impacted on the domestic order. The dichotomy between the aspirations and the tensions of the "national mission" were seen clearly in December 1995 when Turkey acceded to the European Union (EU) Customs Union; in the same month the Islamist Refah (Welfare or Prosperity) Party achieved its most significant electoral successes. In July 1996 the attempt to balance competing images of Turkey's place in the world was seen in the Refah-True Path Party (DYP) coalition government, which brought together the veteran Islamist leader Necmitten Erbakan, with the Westernized, military-supported secularist, Tansu Ciller.

It is the aim of this paper to assess Turkey's post-Cold War security policy to the present day, based on an examination of the foundations and exercise of both Turkey's defense and foreign policies. From this, the paper will assess how far Turkey's security policy has changed since the end of the Cold War, and the implications for its relationship with the West.

Notes

1. Philip Robins, *Turkish Policy in the Gulf Crisis—Adventurist or Dynamic?*, in *Turkish Foreign Policy: New Prospects*, ed. Clement H. Dodd (Wistow, Eothen Press, 1992), 70.

2. In this paper the term "West" is used to refer to both to the geographic concept of the West, the countries of North America and those European countries in NATO and the EU, and to that group of countries bound by a broadly recognizable set of historical, cultural and religious ties.

3. The enthusiasm of this time, regarding the future regional role of Turkey, is illustrated in Paul B. Henze, *Turkey: Toward the Twenty-First Century*, in *Turkey's New Geopolitics* (Boulder: Westview Press, 1993), 1-35. Another study is *Turkey's Strategic Position at the Crossroads of World Affairs* (Carlisle, PA: Strategic Studies Institute, U.S. Army War College, 1993). Like a number of U.S. studies it provides a good overview of Turkey's options in different regions, but under-estimates the constraints on Turkey's actions imposed by geography, economics, and internal structures.

4.   Winston S. Churchill, *The Aftermath* (New York, 1929), 380.

5.   Saul B. Cohen, quoted in Colin S. Gray, "The Continued Primacy of Geography," in *Orbis* 40, no. 2 (Spring 1996): 247.

6.   In 1935 Mustafa Kemal decreed that every Turk would follow the Western practice of adopting a surname. He himself dropped the titles Ghazi and Pasha, and the Arab name Mustafa. He took the name Ataturk, Father of the Turks, and henceforth signed himself Kemal Ataturk. Lord Kinross, *Ataturk: The Rebirth of a Nation* (London: Weidenfeld and Nicholson, 1993), 473-474.

7.   Memorandum by Ahmed Atif, the Reis Effendi, to the divan, 1798, quoted in Ferenc Vali, *Bridge Across the Bosporos* (Baltimore and London: Johns Hopkins University Press, 1971), 42.

2.
Historical Influences on Modern Turkey

The Origins and Legacy of Ottoman Greatness

The death of Suleyman the Magnificent in 1566 saw the Ottoman Empire at the apogee of its vigor and territory, stretching from the Danube to Yemen, from Albania to the Northern shores of the Black Sea, and from Algeria to Baghdad. By the middle of the 16th century, the Ottoman Empire was the dominant Islamic state and the major European, Mediterranean, Middle Eastern, and Persian Gulf power.

In 1055, the Seljuk Turks—Turkoman nomads and military adventurers from Central Asia—forced the Abbasid Caliph of Baghdad to recognize them as the protectors of orthodox Sunni Islam and their leader as Sultan. Expansionists, they advanced into Eastern Anatolia and in 1071 won a decisive victory over the Byzantines at Manzikert, establishing an Islamic presence in Anatolia that has lasted over 1,000 years. The Seljuks brought with them the Turkoman tribe from which sprang the Ottoman dynasty and empire. From 1299, Osman, the Ottoman founder, began a policy of territorial expansion at the expense of the Byzantines, and over the next two centuries Osman's successors consolidated their state, wearing down the residual Byzantine power. In three campaigns the Ottoman state transformed itself into an empire. In 1453, Sultan Mehmet II, "the Conqueror," took Constantinople (hereafter called Istanbul), thereby giving the Ottomans a strategic base from which to dominate the Black Sea and the Eastern

7

Mediterranean and thereby, to the present day, controlling Russian access to the Mediterranean.[1]

The second campaign began as traditional regional and religious competition with the Iranian Shiites. However, Selim I decided instead to confront and neutralize another regional rival, the Mamluk Empire. The Ottoman armies easily defeated the Mamluks and, with the capture of Cairo in 1517, acquired most of the classical heartland of Arab Islam. This success established the Ottomans as supreme within the community of Islam (the *Ummah*). Selim arrogated to himself the title of Caliph and assumed responsibility for protection of the Holy Cities of Mecca and Medina. In turn, his son, Suleyman the Magnificent, added to this empire Hungary, Transylvania, Tripoli, Algiers, Iraq, Rhodes, Eastern Anatolia, part of Georgia, the most important Aegean Islands, and Belgrade, from which base he besieged Vienna. In addition he turned the Empire into a formidable naval power.

This pre-eminent position lasted for over 200 years, until Ottoman power began to decline in the middle of the 18th century as the internal structures of the empire proved impervious to necessary reform, and the growing military strength of the European powers led to permanent territorial losses. The empire finally collapsed in 1918 but the memory of imperial greatness remained a significant element in the psychology and actions of the Republic of Turkey and of the former territories of the Empire. Despite antagonism between modern Turkey and former subjects, the climax of Ottoman power would be recognized by Muslims as the last time Islam dealt with the West on equal terms.

The Ottomans and the West

There was contact between the Ottomans and the West from the start, and the Islamic basis of Ottoman power defined the relationship with Western Europe as one of antagonism and conflict. However, defeat in the Russian Wars of 1768-1774, leading to the first permanent loss of Muslim-held territory, changed the dynamics of the relationship. Defeat starkly demonstrated that Ottoman armies were no longer well enough organized, equipped, trained, or led to compete against contemporary Western armies. The conclusion drawn was that military competition with the West was only possible by adopting Western military methods and technology. This represented compromise of historical proportions, because the close identification between the "West" and Christianity made accommodation extremely difficult. The strains set up between those who advocated the adoption of European techniques and those who viewed any dismantling of the Islamic order as heresy should not be underestimated. However, the Sultan was also Caliph and therefore, unlike in Iran, the religious establishment (the *ulema*) had less influence and control over temporal issues.

At the same time, the French Revolution introduced two major influences with lasting impact on the development of modern Turkey: secularism, the conscious separation of state and religion; and nationalism, the concept of the identification of the state with a recognizably homogenous ethnic group. Secularism had little impact until Ataturk, but nationalism acted almost immediately on the non-Muslim ethnic groups in Ottoman society. It was first seized on by the Greeks and other Christian minorities, but even Muslim Albanians soon sought their own state, and ultimately the Arab subject peoples put a sense of nationalism above loyalty to the Sultan-Caliph. This disillusioning process of desertion was in time matched by a process of growing nationalism among the ethnic Turkish groups in the empire.

Military reforms were designed to be stand-alone measures, aimed at restoring the military balance on the Ottoman borders. Inevitably they brought in their wake foreign advisers, new educational methods, language requirements, permanent diplomatic missions in great power capitals, loans, and commercial agreements. In addition this led to the development of a new elite, "the French Knowers," providing the Ottoman state with their eyes and ears on the West. The majority of this class were drawn from the *devsirme,* Christian or Jewish converts to Islam, who were more responsive to Western influence. In the middle years of the 19th century, an era known as the *Tanzimat* (Reorganization), the pace of reform reached its most intensive, and the primacy of this new elite in the bureaucracy opened many nonmilitary areas to European reforms. Although such "Westerners" did not openly question the Islamic foundation of society, their policies further reduced the institutional significance of the *ulema.*

To add to the Ottoman problems, reform did not come cheap. Military reorganization was financed by loans, as were many other reform activities. This, allied to the historical granting of tax exemptions to European traders and trading communities, the "capitulations,"[2] further hamstrung Ottoman attempts to raise revenue or balance the budget. In 1876 the Ottoman Government failed on debt repayments and surrendered financial independence. The Europeans set up the humiliating Public Debt Administration that gave debt repayment priority over all other Ottoman expenditures at a time when the empire was struggling for its existence. The aggressive statism and attempts at autarky under Ataturk and his successors had their origins in these bitter economic humiliations.

The Ottomans and the European Balance of Power

It is unlikely that the Ottomans could have reversed decline whatever reform measures they undertook. That it took until the defeat of World War I finally to shatter the structure was largely because of the European balance of power politics. While the Great Powers had lost their own fear of the Ottomans, each saw any progressive weakening as part of a zero-sum game with the other empires. This equation lay at the heart of what was referred to as "the Eastern Question." The Ottomans also played the game. Referring to Ottoman security policy, Ahmed Atif wrote, "The permanent policy of the Empire is to prevent any increase in the strength of Russia and Austria, which by virtue of their position are its natural enemies, and to be allied with those states which might be able to break their power and are thus the natural friends of the Empire."[3]

This assessment had important parallels in the security policy of the Republic of Turkey. It was defensive and reactive, it identified Russia as the primary threat, and it looked to alliances, regional arrangements, and balances of power for support. It reflected a recognition that the Ottomans had moved from "Great Power" to "Small Power" status, in other words "a state (or empire) that recognizes it cannot obtain security primarily by use of its own capabilities, and that it must rely fundamentally on the aid of other states, institutions, processes or developments of their own."[4] Hence, although the developing democracies of Britain and France were antagonistic to the Ottomans, as Muslims and autocrats, their equal antipathy to Russia and Austria-Hungary, combined with their imperial responsibilities and ambitions, gave them a vested interest in supporting the Ottomans against unilateral expansion in the region. At the Paris Peace Conference of 1856, which ended the Crimean War, the Ottomans were therefore admitted as participants, in a grudging acknowledgment of the "European" dimension of their power.

This was the high water mark of European accommodation with the Ottomans. The 1878 Congress of Berlin, called once again to limit Russian expansion at Ottoman expense, did not include them, and they received support only by agreeing to further territorial concessions. This Great Power consensus did not last long. As Ottoman power in the Balkans collapsed, even real-politick support for the Ottomans evaporated, to be replaced by a sense of moral outrage at the atrocities that marked this period.[5] A belief grew that the Ottomans were now doomed, and that the best option was to move into the most advantageous position to profit from it.

The Development of Turkish Nationalism

In the face of decline, three broad strands of thought appeared in the Empire, each with an important influence on the development of modern Turkey, each with the same basic aim: regeneration of the state. These were Ottomanism,[6] Turkism, and Islamism. The first would disintegrate in the face of aggressive nationalism. A narrowly defined version of the second would triumph with Ataturk's success in forging a new state out of imperial disaster. Islamism was discarded by Ataturk, but it could not be eradicated and sustained itself to the present day as an alternative to the state's constitutionally avowed secularism.

The term "Turk" carried derogatory overtones for both Europeans and the educated Ottoman elite. However, in the tribulations of the 19th century many people looked to the ethnic origins of imperial greatness and drew lessons from the militant nationalism among Ottoman subject peoples. Therefore the concept of Turkism began to gather appeal. At first the concept of "Turkism" was identified more generally with Pan-Turkism, a union of all Turkish and Turkic peoples, not only throughout the empire but also in the Caucasus, Central Asia, and across to Western China. This brand of Turkism reached its high-water mark in 1921-1922, with Enver Pasha's attempts to rally the Turkic peoples of Central Asia against Soviet attempts to re-establish Russian hegemony in the region. His death effectively ended realistic hopes for Pan-Turkism for nearly 70 years. The collapse of the Soviet Union in 1991 revived it, providing a potent new focus for Turkish security policy in the post-Cold War era.

Ultimately, the more effective brand of Turkism was that of a narrower Turkish nationalism that concentrated on Anatolia as the Turkish and Ottoman heartland. It was to be adopted by Ataturk as one of the defining pillars of what came to be known as Kemalism, and it gained enormous strength from the prodigious efforts of Anatolian Turks during the War of Independence. In the face of defeat by Europe and rejection by

12

former subjects, it struck an increasingly powerful and popular chord.[7] Allied to the appeal of Turkish nationalism, Ataturk propagated a concept of citizenship within a constitutional state where the term "Turk" would designate a "citizen" of the new Turkish state, not denote ethnic origin. His slogan, "Happy the man who calls himself a Turk," was designed to emphasize this new loyalty, although the strains this would raise in the Kurdish areas of Southeast Anatolia would show that such an ideology was not strong enough to offset the demands of an ethnic solidarity based on language and culture.

The most effective spokesman of this ideology was Mehmet Ziya Gokalp.[8] He was an ardent supporter of political ideas that emphasized the supremacy of the state over the individual, and he believed passionately that the ethnic "nation" was the natural political and social unit. In Gokalp's definition, the "nation" were those people who spoke the same language, had the same education, and were united in their religious, moral and aesthetic ideals.[9] Ataturk would adopt a very similar definition, but as a staunch advocate of secularism, he would drop the element of religion. Gokalp's thinking was encapsulated in his slogan: "We belong to the Turkish nation, the Muslim religious community, and the European civilization."[10]

In this he drew a bold distinction between "civilization," a rational system of knowledge, science, and technology; and "culture," the set of values, habits and conditions current in a community. His role model was Japan, which had so successfully embraced Western "civilization" during the 19th century that in 1905 its navy annihilated the Russians at Tsushima. The acceptance of Japan by the European powers as "one of us" was evidence to Gokalp and Ataturk that non-Christian countries could enter the circle of Western civilization and that religion was not necessarily a pre-condition of acceptance. In his poem *Esnaf Destam* he says:

We were defeated because we were so backward,
To take revenge, we shall adopt the enemy's science.
We shall learn his skill, steal his methods.
On progress we shall set our heart.
We shall skip five hundred years and we shall not stand still.
Little time is left.[11]

World War One And Defeat

In 1914 the Ottomans entered World War One on the side of the Central Powers. Like other powers faced with seemingly intractable internal and external problems, they saw their solution in military decision. They were defeated.[12] However, three features of the struggle need mentioning for their long-term influence on modern Turkey's relations with the outside world. First was the Allied process of "expansionist bookings-in-advance,"[13] which culminated in the 1920 Treaty of Sevres. This confirmed the Turkish impression of ingrained, vindictive Western hostility, fueling resistance in the War of Independence, and leaving a smouldering resentment and suspicion of the West, despite Ataturk's hopes. Second, despite enormous losses, the Ottomans' German-trained army operated much more effectively than the Allies expected. Despite defeat, the Turkish Army and some of its leaders, notably Ataturk, emerged from the conflict with professional pride and reputation intact.

Third, in operations against the Russians, the Ottoman Government adopted a policy of securing its rear areas by wholesale expulsion of the pro-Russian Armenians. Whether as a result of a deliberate policy of genocide, as claimed by the Armenians, or local ill-discipline and poor administration in appalling weather conditions, as claimed by the Turks, probably over a million Armenians died. Christian sympathy for these events fueled a substantial, long-lasting body of anti-Turkish feeling in the West.[14]

On 31 October 1918 the Sultan signed an unconditional surrender. The Ottomans thought they were signing on the basis of President Wilson's Fourteen Points, including that of national self-determination. In fact, with no regard for any *Turkish* national claims, the whole empire had already been partitioned between the Allies, as had most of the Anatolian heartland of the Ottomans. The formulation of a comprehensive postwar settlement for the Ottoman Empire was so complex that the terms of a settlement were only finalized in the 1920 Treaty of Sevres. Stripped of its empire, it was intended that an Ottoman state and government remain but that it would be severely circumscribed. The Straits were put under the jurisdiction of an international commission,[15] Greece was given Thrace, in addition to sharing Anatolia with Italy and France. In addition, the Treaty recognized an independent Armenian state and a semi-autonomous Kurdish state in Eastern Anatolia.

The War of Independence and the National Pact

Before the ink was dry on the paper, the terms of the settlement had been overtaken by events. Occupation had a profound effect on the Turkish population of Anatolia, many of whom had already suffered dispossession from former areas of the Ottoman Empire. In disgust at the Istanbul Government's craven submission to Allied will, societies for "the defense of rights" sprang up to contest the occupation and division of Turkish soil, particularly by the hated Greeks. The movement had its focus, inspiration and leadership in the person of Ataturk. Churchill's judgment on Ataturk should be quoted in full to give some measure of the moment and the man:

> Loaded with follies, stained with crimes, rotted with misgovernment, shattered by battle, worn down by long disastrous wars, his empire falling to pieces around him, the Turk was still alive. In his breast was beating the heart of a race that had challenged the world, and for centuries had contended victoriously against all comers. In his hands was once again the equipment of a modern army, and at his head a Captain, who with all that is learned of him, ranks among

the four or five outstanding figures of the cataclysm. In the tapestried and gilded chambers of Paris were assembled the law-givers of the world. In Constantinople, under the guns of the Allied fleets, there functioned a puppet Government of Turkey. But among the stern hills and valleys of "the Turkish Homelands" in Anatolia, there dwelt that company of poor men . . . who would not see it settled so; and at their bivouac fires at this moment sat, in the rags of a refugee, the August Spirit of Fair Play.[16]

Ataturk not only led military operations against the occupiers but also sought to harness the new, but ardent, nationalism to an organization that could replace Istanbul as the legitimate representative of that new, politically distinct body, "the Turkish People." In April 1920, 4 months before Sevres was even signed, Ataturk was elected President of the new Grand National Assembly (GNA) in Ankara. In January 1921 the GNA adopted a constitution that contained the National Pact.[17] The Pact acknowledged the loss of the Balkans and renounced outright any territorial claims to former Arab provinces, but affirmed the right of full Turkish sovereignty over those remaining portions of the Empire inhabited by Turkish majorities. It has remained the basis of Turkish foreign policy ever since.

In 1921 the Turks and the new Soviet Russian Government crushed the nascent Armenian state. Ataturk now smashed the Greeks at the battle of Sakarya and by September 1922 had ejected the Greeks from Anatolia. Ataturk was prepared to go to war with Britain to enforce the demands of the National Pact but Britain's heart did not lie in further conflict. The parties agreed to renegotiate the Treaty of Sevres, and this was achieved with the Treaty of Lausanne (24 July 1923). With the exception of Mosul in Northern Iraq, the Province of Hatay (containing Antioch and the port of Iskendrum), and the placing of the Bosphorus and Dardenelles Straits under international supervision, Turkish sovereignty was recognized over all areas claimed in the National Pact.

16

Conclusion

The influence of the heroic nature of the struggle for the independence of the new Turkish state cannot be overstated. From imperial collapse, partition and occupation in 1920 it emerged 3 years later as the internationally recognized, independent, nation-state of the Republic of Turkey.[18] Turkey therefore began its existence stripped of an empire, but conscious of imperial greatness and now defined by a strong national identity based on the military reversal of Great Power impositions and the rallying cry of "Turk." The Ottoman tradition of the closest identification of the military with the state continued, giving the armed forces a pre-eminent role in society. In time, not only would they remain defenders of the Republic, they would also arrogate to themselves the guardianship of Kemalism, Ataturk's legacy to Turkey.

Turkey's relationship with the outside world was to be characterized by a prickly, aggressive defensiveness. However, despite the revisionist nature of his struggle against the European powers, Ataturk was determined to align Turkey with the West. The relationship would remain ambiguous for a long time. Ataturk saw the future of national development in the adoption of Western practices, yet the Turkish people were aware of strong European and Christian antipathy. The division between the reformist, Western-oriented, secular elite, and the Islamic, conservative rural majority remained. Relations with Turkey's Balkan and Armenian neighbors ranged from dislike to loathing, although the entry of transiently friendly Soviet Russia into the equation did much to balance this. The "mandate" status of the new Arab states did not allow them to deal with Turkey as equals until after World War Two, and although they shared an Ottoman and an Islamic heritage, the former master-vassal relationship and ethnic differences continued to color their relationship. Most significantly, those who had contributed least to the foundation of the new Republic, the Istanbul establishment, were the most enthusiastic supporters of Ataturk's aspirations, while those who had done most, the Anatolian peasantry, accepted them,

17

not out of understanding or conviction but because it was Ataturk's wish.

How all these factors would manifest themselves in the foreign and defense policies of the new Republic would lie largely in the hands of Ataturk, whose personification of the struggle for independence gave him a primacy in the new Republic that was broadly unchallenged. Secure within the boundaries of the new state, he set about one of the most dramatic transformations of civil society yet seen.

Notes

1. A most comprehensive study of the origins and history of the Ottomans is in Stanford J. Shaw and Ezel Kural Shaw, *History of the Ottoman Empire and Modern Turkey* , 2 vols. (Gateshead: Cambridge University Press, 1977; reprinted 1994).

2. An idea of the extensive nature of the privileges can be seen in Shaw, *History of Ottoman Empire,* vol.1, 97-98 and 163-164.

3. Quoted in quoted in Ferenc Vali, *Bridge Across the Bosporos* (Baltimore and London: Johns Hopkins University Press, 1971), 42.

4. Robert L. Rothstein, *Alliances and Small Powers* (New York and London: Columbia University Press, 1968), 29.

5. These were what Gladstone referred to as the "Bulgarian Horrors" when he called on Britain to eject "the unspeakable Turk . . . one and all, bag and baggage" from Europe. Speech in Parliament 7 May 1877.

6. Feroz Ahmad, *The Making of Modern Turkey* (London and New York: Routledge, 1993), 34, and Erik J. Zurcher, *Turkey, A Modern History* (London and New York: I.B. Taurus, 1993), 133. Also Shaw, *History of Ottoman Empire,* 127-128 and 288-289.

7. Shaw, *History of Ottoman Empire,* 260-263, and William L. Cleveland, *A History of the Modern Middle East* (Boulder: Westview Press, 1994), 130-131.

8. Ziya Gokalp's (1876-1924) background, career and writings are covered in Shaw, *History of Ottoman Empire.* His importance lay in giving Turkish nationalism an intellectual framework. The contemporary relevance of his thought comes through clearly in his own book *Turkish Nationalism and Western Civilisation* (London: Allen and Unwin, 1959).

9. Uriel Heyd, *Foundations of Turkish Nationalism, The Life and Teachings of Ziya Gokalp* (London: Luzac & Company, 1950), 63.

10. Ibid., 149.

11. Ibid., 79.

12. There are many books on the Ottoman involvement in World War One, particularly covering the Gallipoli Campaign. Shaw, *History of the Ottoman Empire*, vol. 2, 310-328, gives a good summary of the Ottoman struggle. Lord Kinross, *Ataturk: The Rebirth of a Nation* (London: Weidenfeld and Nicholson, 1993), 473-474, covers Ataturk's achievements during the World War.

13. Elizabeth Monroe, *Britain's Moment in the Middle East, 1914-1971* (London: 1981), 26.

14. The conflicting arguments in this highly emotive issue are set out well in Gwynne Dyer, *Turkish "Falsifiers" and Armenian "Deceivers": Historiography and the Armenian Massacres,* Middle Eastern Studies 12, 1976. Despite attempts by the newly independent Republic of Armenia to reach a *modus vivendi* with its Turkish neighbor, the Armenian Diaspora, who are very influential in America, keep the historical enmity alive. Every year they attempt to get 24 April designated as Genocide Day. This is an intense irritation for the Turks, who refuse to accept responsibility for events that took place under the Ottomans. Shaw, who has publicly disputed the Armenian figures, was on the "hit list" of ASALA, the Armenian terrorist group.

15. In 1915 the Straits had been offered to Russia to encourage it to remain in the War. Fortunately, in 1917 Lenin sanctimoniously renounced all agreements with the Allies. The most comprehensive survey of the place of the Straits in international politics is probably Ferenc A. Vali, *The Turkish Straits and NATO* (Stanford: Hoover Institution Studies, 1972).

16. Quoted in Kinross, *Ataturk,* 184.

17. The National Pact was issued on 17 February 1920 by the last Ottoman Parliament. It represented the nationalists' belief that it was "the maximum of sacrifice . . . to achieve a just and lasting peace." Shaw, *History of Ottoman Empire*, 347-348.

18. On 1 November 1922 the Grand National Assembly (GNA) separated the Sultanate and the Caliphate, abolishing the former. On 3 March 1924 the GNA abolished the Caliphate. This marked the formal end of the Ottoman Empire, almost 640 years from Osman's foundation of the dynasty.

3.
The State Foundations of Turkish Security Policy

Geopolitical Foundations

Despite the changed world of 1923, the Republic of Turkey could not dissociate itself from its Ottoman heritage. New Turkey inherited the geographical essentials of the Empire, the most important feature being control of the Straits. This vital sea passage remained the only access for the Soviet Union to warm waters in winter, and despite the provisions for international supervision, Ataturk's war had ensured that Turkey continued to command both sides of the channel. This alone guaranteed that modern Turkey could not be dismissed as a Middle Eastern country.

The small area of the Straits and European Thrace was both strategically and psychologically important, but also very vulnerable to attack. However, the Anatolian part of Turkey was highly defensible. On three sides there were seas (the Black, Aegean, and Mediterranean), and in the east protection was offered by the mountains of the Kurdish region and the Armenian highlands. The border with the Soviet Union now ran along the foot of high mountains inside Turkey. Only the border with Syria was less defensible, but this lay away from Turkey's political capital, transferred, for strategic and cultural reasons, from Istanbul to Ankara.[1]

Secure in its Anatolian heartland, it would often be the water-related issues that would be the focus of Turkey's security concerns. These included continuing competition for

21

control of the Straits, the Greek control of the majority of the Aegean islands, the status of the island of Cyprus with its Turkish minority, and the fact that Iraq and Syria both drew their irrigation water supplies from the Tigris and Euphrates, whose headwaters rise in Turkey.

Ethnic Foundations

The disruption of the war had been massive. Most non-Muslims were gone, with the Greek population reduced from 1.8 million to 120,000, and the Armenian from 1.3 million to 100,000. Two and one-half million Turks had died, leaving a population of about 13.3 million in Thrace and Anatolia.[2] The majority of this population had Islam in common, but ethnic, religious and linguistic homogeneity did not exist. The population was of mixed descent, a fact recognized by Ataturk in seeking to bind them together with his concept of "Turk" as a citizen. Despite the emphasis on Turkish nationalism, only a small proportion of the population was actually related to the original Seljuks, most being "Anatolians" descended from the peoples who had inhabited Asia Minor from prehistoric times, and others assimilated over the centuries under the Ottomans. In addition there were the immigration influxes from the Balkans, Caucasus, and Middle East. Ethnic minorities no longer had such political significance, but there were two important sources of potential upheaval, the Kurds[3] and the Alewites (or Alevis).[4]

Ideological Foundations

Under the Eastern Roman Empire and the Byzantines, the scope of "Europe" was not seen as ending on the Northern shore of the Bosphorus. Toynbee wrote, "The historian cannot lay a finger on any period....in which there was any significant cultural diversity between the "Asiatic" and "European" occupants of the all but contiguous banks of a Bosphorus and a Hellespont."[5] It was Islam that destroyed this geographical definition, introducing a religio-ideological division that anchored "Europe" north of the Straits. Jacob Burckhardt, writing about reforms in Russia, asserted, "The Russian element at least *can* flow into European civilization because it has no Koran."[6] It was Ataturk's remarkable mission to attempt to shape the new state so that, despite history and the Islamic nature of Turkish society, modern Turkey, too, would be in a position to "flow into European civilization."

The experience of state-building has an important bearing on the political culture of a country. In defining states, R. N. Berki drew a useful distinction between transcendentalism, or "statist orientation," and instrumentalism, or "societal orientation."[7] In transcendentalism, the community has priority over the members; its "interest" is greater than the aggregate of the interests of the members; the association is based on uniformity; the law is seen as the expression of the collective will of the membership; politics is understood primarily in terms of leadership and education. Transcendentalism connotes the high ideals of duty, service and sublimation of energy to a higher cause.

In instrumentalism, association does not necessarily have a moral dimension, only common interests; law is conceived of in terms of rational agreement among members; politics is seen in terms of the reconciliation of interests. Instrumentalism connotes freedom, diversity, and plurality.

Berki therefore categorizes most Western states as "moderate instrumental" polities, while Turkey has been for the most part a "moderate transcendental" polity. This distinction helps explain why Turkey views itself the way it does, and how it formulates and exercises its security policy. It also helps to explain why Turkey has difficulties satisfying the requirements of democratic government, as the West defines the term.

Ataturk founded the Republic on the basis of a single, overriding national mission: the elevation of the Turkish people to the level of contemporary civilization, identified as that of the West. The goals were national security based on territorial integrity and full sovereignty, and the modernization of society. This orientation to the West was a conscious

23

continuation of the late Ottoman policy. It was not based on any romantic attachment to the West; Ataturk and his peers had spent their professional lives defending the Ottoman Empire, and then the Republic, against Western predations. It was a hardhearted, practical decision based on the fact that the West represented success and that only by achieving those standards would Turkey be accepted as an equal. Initially, the Western orientation remained philosophical and technical, designed to gain acceptance and to modernize, but after World War Two the relationship took on strong military and security dimensions.

The challenge was to balance the demands of the religious, ethnic, and cultural aspects of society, with the ideological commitment to Western "civilization," while at the same time defending against external threats. This meant that the internal organization, and the external foreign policy of Turkey, would be bound together inextricably from the outset. Under the Ottomans the maxim had been "no power without an army, and no army without power." Under Ataturk, domestic policy, in the broadest sense, would aim at securing and achieving the national mission, while security policy would ensure the external and internal conditions under which domestic policy could succeed.

In a transcendental polity, it falls to the leader to identify the path of progress and determine the policies to achieve this. Therefore, "Ataturk took up a non-existent, hypothetical entity, the Turkish nation, and breathed life into it. . . . Whenever a rationale was invoked for his moves, the reason given was that of the "requirements of contemporary civilization."[8] Reforms were imposed from above, and modern Turkey developed under the tutelage of Ataturk and a small, determined elite. Ideological guidance came from the implementation of the principles embodied in the "Six Arrows" of Kemalism, adopted by the Republican Peoples Party (CHP)[9] in 1931 and endorsed within the Constitution in 1937.[10] These principles were: nationalism, secularism, republicanism, populism, statism, and reformism. Each carried within it both domestic and foreign policy implications.

Nationalism was synonymous with the narrow definition of Turkism, rejecting both irredentist Ottoman inclinations and expansionist pan-Turkist ambitions. *Secularism* aimed at the separation of state and religion, denying a leading role to Islam, thereby seeking to make religion the disestablished, private affair it was in much of the West. *Republicanism* was directed against the re-establishment of the Sultan and Caliph, attracting the applause of some European republicans, although dismaying many Muslims both within and outside Turkey. *Populism* contained elements of Ottomanism, embracing the equality of all citizens, and suggestive of a democratic form of government. *Statism* meant concentration of the economy in government hands—a reaction against the foreign economic domination in the Ottoman era, but also implying development, and economic and technological assimilation with the West. *Reformism* implied the dynamic transformation of the Turkish state and society, in line with Ataturk's ideological commitment to the West.

State, Society, and the Formulation of Foreign Policy

The Ottoman Empire had been a militant entity that institutionalized a strong state tradition that encouraged a "recognition of the state's absolute right to legislate on public matters."[11] Unlike Western European states where functional, horizontal divisions developed in society, with economic and social classes developing common identities and mores, Ottoman society was more apt to cleave vertically. When the center was weak the periphery would not act as organized classes seeking to share state power, but as individuals striving to increase personal power and wealth. What had developed was a division of society between the elite (the leadership and the wealthy), intermediaries (the civil and military bureaucracies), and the masses (largely peasants). This political culture continued under the Republic where the social structure was autocratic and this reflected in politics, the army, school and the family. There was a continuing admiration of strength, and leaders were expected to exercise protection and patronage for their supporters. Consultation and the delegation of authority were rare and all important issues were decided at the highest level. Vociferous expressions of public opinion often served to disguise the lack of influence over decisionmaking, particularly in the arena of defense and foreign policy.[12] The emphasis on statism for economic development, and a cultural suspicion and distrust of businessmen and entrepreneurs, continually hampered the growth of a politically significant economic middle class, and hence development of the economy itself. In this environment the position and role of the bureaucratic elites of the civil service and the army were enormously important.[13] This elite was not homogenous. The Ministry of Foreign Affairs (MFA) continued to bear a strong intellectual and social resemblance to their Ottoman forebears, the military were more often intelligent lower middle class or peasants, whose education and status came from being in the military. Their attachment to the national mission was absolute: the civil service from conviction, the military because Ataturk had charged them with it.

The Civil Service

Under the Ottomans the civil service bureaucracy, initially dependent totally on the Sultan, developed an independence as the Sultans became weaker. This had become particularly marked during the Tanzimat reform era, when the bureaucratic elite began to see themselves as servants of an autonomous "state" and not the Sultan, and sought to initiate and implement reform and foreign policy, by the light of their own priorities. This reformist tendency among this small educated elite was reinforced by adoption of the so-called "cast-iron" theory of Islam, which Ataturk also subscribed to, whereby

Islam had fallen out of phase with life and could no longer be adapted to modern circumstances.[14] Therefore, in addition to a weak civil society, the Turkish Republic inherited from the Ottomans a strong attachment to the state and an arrogant, secular bureaucratic elite that continued to see the state as autonomous from "society." This did have advantages in the early years where "Experience in statecraft, respect for the state, the importance of the state in Turkish culture, have all been specific, steadying factors in the history of the Turkish Republic, endowing it with a degree of political gravitas, absent from most new countries."[15] This psychology was particularly strong in the professional diplomatic corps of the MFA, who had embraced Ataturk's foreign policy assumptions wholeheartedly and subscribed fully to the national mission. Ataturk's political priorities did not challenge the position of the civil service, and the dramatic social revolution disguised the slow growth of civil society. Turkish society remained authoritarian, traditional and elitist, with political power concentrated at the top.

The Army

The war had been a national struggle, and the army had gained heroic status as defender of the nation. Ataturk, by his pre-eminence, crucially secured the loyalty of the army to himself and the Republic. The constitution of 1924 made the Chief of the Turkish General Staff (TGS) directly responsible to the president and vested supreme command of the armed forces in the GNA, "as represented by the person of the President of the Republic."[16] However, with victory secure the army was left in an ambiguous position. On the one hand Ataturk wanted to keep the military out of the political system, while on the other he continued to look to the army as the ultimate guardian of his achievements. In 1923 the Assembly passed a law that military men must resign from the army before standing for election. Later the Military Penal Code made it an offense for any member of the armed forces to join a political party or to take part in political activity.

In 1931, Ataturk urged younger officers to think of themselves as at the forefront of the development of Turkey: "The Turkish nation has always seen its army . . . as the permanent vanguard in movements to achieve lofty national ideals. . . . The Turkish nation considers its army to be the guardian of its ideals."[17] A vital function of the army was to be one of the regime's most important agents for the spread of the ideas of modernization and secular nationalism, especially among conscripts. This indoctrination in a radical reformist consciousness was reinforced by the system of military education, a system many of Turkey's elite went through. In 1935 the Army Internal Service Law formally spelled out that the "duty of the armed forces is to protect and defend the Turkish homeland and the Turkish Republic, as determined in the Constitution." This was interpreted as an imposition by law to defend Turkey against internal as well as external threats, further institutionalizing the belief that the achievement of the national mission was dependent on the inseparability of domestic and foreign policy. The military thus had at its core the same transcendental aspect as the state, developing an identity and mission inspired by the achievements of Ataturk and dedicated to their maintenance.[18]

The Army was fortunate not to face major external challenges to Turkey in the early years. Until well into the Second World War the Army was an under-resourced, outdated, and questionably effective organization, suited only to internal security. Its equipment was 80 percent German from the previous war, the rest being donated by the Russians or taken from the Greeks. Partly re-equipped by the Allies toward the end of World War Two, the real drive for modernization did not begin until 1947, under the Truman Doctrine. General Pendleton, who led the U.S. Military Aid Mission in Ankara over this period, said, "From the late 1940s to the mid-1950s we built up the Turkish Army from scratch."[19] The total dependence of Turkey on U.S. arms continued until the 1970s.

There was no national plan, and Turkey simply took what it was given, according to what the United States had, or was replacing, at the time. The 1975 U.S. arms embargo in the wake of the Cyprus intervention was a great shock, but it also alerted Turkey to the eclectic, obsolete, and unstructured nature of the armed forces it had developed. Under the military government of 1980-1983, the TGS initiated the REMO (Reorganization-Modernization) project.

The Role of the Army in Security Policy

While Turkey remained a single-party state there was coincidence of interest among the army, the state, and the government. In 1946 President Inonu consulted the military over the decision to allow the establishment of opposition parties, assuring them that a multiparty system would pose no threat to Ataturk's reforms and that the military would continue to be the custodian of the state. In the postwar period the military fully supported the foreign policy objectives of President Bayar, who was deeply hostile to the Soviet Union, viewed neutralism as immoral, and followed Inonu's lead in aligning Turkey firmly with the West militarily and economically. They also supported the development of particularly strong links with the United States. In strategic matters, as in defense procurement, most decisions were led by U.S. and NATO planners. The Democratic Party (DP) government of 1950-1960, which broke the monopoly of the Ataturkist CHP, was also broadly supportive of these foreign policy objectives. However, in domestic issues Prime Minister Menderes polarized politics, trying to use popular support in an increasingly radical manner to outflank the state tradition represented by the bureaucratic elite. In 1960 the military felt impelled to intervene on the basis of a "sense of national mission." Turan explained the pattern of military intervention in this instance and those of 1971 and 1980:

> In each of the instances in which the Turkish Armed Forces have assumed political power, their intervention has been

29

preceded by intensifying disregard for . . . political democracy by the ruling parties . . . and escalating political polarization. . . . On each occasion, the coming to power of the military has been met with relief by the general electorate. . . . The military leadership often send warning signals. . . . Yet the intensity of the conflict causes these warning signals to go unheeded. Then the military assumes political power directly and indirectly.[20]

The direct result of the 1960 intervention was a new constitution that formalized the military role in the formulation of security policy. Although the 1961 Constitution gave the GNA responsibility for foreign affairs, in reality power came to rest in the National Security Council (NSC), which was set up specifically to ensure agreement between the politicians and the military on security issues, before they entered the public domain. It was headed by the President and contained the Chief of TGS and all the Service Chiefs. It was charged with preparing national security plans and programs, coordinating national security activities, and "offering information" to the Council of Ministers. There are no recorded instances of NSC decisions ever being overturned. In the "Coup by Memorandum" of 1971, the NSC role was further strengthened and empowered to "advise" the Council. The memorandum itself held the GNA and the government responsible for dragging the country into anarchy and unrest and claimed that the public had lost hope of reaching the level of contemporary civilization set as a goal for Turks by Ataturk.[21]

Throughout this period the army remained unpoliticized and autonomous, while increasingly seeing its mission as the guardian of the national interest. This ambiguous role meant that since 1961 "politics has always been under the scrutiny of the military; it (Turkey) has not been a completely autonomous liberal democracy."[22] The Chief of TGS was appointed directly by the president and reported to the prime minister, not the minister of defense. In the NSC, certain key decisions required not just consultation with the military but their consent. Questions of peace and war, such as intervention in Cyprus, and basic alliances with foreign states could not be concluded without military agreement. The divergence of security priorities between Turkey and its Western allies over the Cyprus issue not only exposed the government to criticism but also convinced TGS of the need for a "national strategy."

In 1974, for the first time, TGS drew up a "National Military Strategic Concept." They carried out the threat assessment entirely on their own, based on intelligence from their own sources. The civilian ministries of the MFA and the minister of defense (MOD) had almost no say in this assessment, on the National Strategic Goals falling out from it, or the Force Goals that TGS then set. In addition, the military resisted supervision of their budget. TGS, with their responsibility for national and internal security, drew up their requirements and submitted them to the MOD. He presented them to the Defense Commission of the GNA, and the GNA was expected to vote them through. The 1982 Constitution strengthened this position.

Foreign Policy and Public Opinion

Despite the continuing strength of the state tradition, the period 1961 to 1980 was one of great social and economic change in Turkey. The 1961 Constitution had been designed to put the military and bureaucratic elite back in a position of primacy with regard to politics, but equally it contained very liberal provisions regarding the press and media. Until 1960 foreign policy had been accepted as a "national policy," determined by the president and the "elite." In spite of some vocal minorities, the unanimous support of the "nation" on security matters was assumed. A Turkish proverb captures the minimal effect of public opinion on policy: "The dog barks but the caravan moves on." From this period the presidents were less powerful or charismatic. There was increased liberalization of the domestic political system, which coincided with a relaxation in international tension, while the real and emotional issues regarding Cyprus at last brought public opinion to bear on foreign policy options, which the state could not ignore. In the GNA both Cyprus and the question of the Turkish-American relationship became occasions for acrimonious debate. The broad thrust of Turkish foreign policy remained consistent, reflecting continuing support for orientation to the West, but the move of foreign policy issues into the domestic, public arena marked a new departure.

The 1980 Intervention and the 1982 Constitution

Ataturk had intended Kemalism to be a framework within which Turkey would identify the way towards the national mission, led and guided by the elite. After his death, "guardianship" of Kemalism became the touchstone of power, and therefore Kemalism moved from being a technique to an ideology. The key issue had now become preservation of Ataturk's reforms and not consolidation of democracy in Turkey. The decreasing usefulness of certain aspects of Kemalism meant that "part of the current malaise in Turkish political culture is due to the fact that the Kemalist paradigm is exhausted . . . and that no successor has been accepted."[23] Writing after the 1980 military intervention Tachau was more specific:

> the legitimating formula (of Kemalism) . . . came under considerable strain. Of the main tenets . . . two remained unchallenged (republicanism and nationalism) . . . two became controversial (secularism and populism) and two became the subject of heated debate and fundamental disagreement (reformism and statism).[24]

Narrow nationalism was soon to be challenged as well. Throughout the 1970s Turkish politics polarized again, this time over the issues of Cyprus and the European Community, education and economic policies, and martial law and corruption. By 1980 there were economic breakdown, civil violence, political terrorism, and Kurdish separatism, and open challenges to the secular basis of society by Islamists. On 12 September 1980 the army intervened for the third time to "re-establish democracy."

On the morning of the coup the army issued a statement setting out the reasons for intervention:

> The aim of the operation is to safeguard the integrity of the country . . . to re-establish the existence and authority of the state, and to eliminate the factors that hinder the smooth working of the democratic order.[25]

Shortly after, General Evren publicly reiterated the military's perception of itself as the most patriotic institution in society:

> I have stated that the Turkish Armed Forces would never allow the Turkish Republic, . . to be taken over by traitors. . . . The sole raison d'être of the Turkish Armed Forces is to defend the country as an indivisible whole against its internal as well as its external enemies, and to see that this country will always be secure.[26]

Under the 1982 Constitution, the Council of Ministers was now obliged to consider "with priority, the decisions of the NSC concerning necessary measures for the protection and independence of the State, the unity and indivisibility of the country, and the peace and security of society."[27] Of equal interest was the military's attempt to undercut the Islamists by extending the state's competence in religious affairs, while at the same time banning any declared Islamic parties. Turgut Ozal, the architect of economic reform under the military regime, swept up much of the Islamic vote under the banner of his broadly based Motherland Party (ANAP).

A New Era

The 1982 Constitution was backed by an overwhelming majority in a referendum, as was General Evren's election as president.[28] In 1983, in an election limited by the army to three parties, ANAP took 41 percent of the vote and 53 percent of GNA seats. This was not the military's choice, but they had returned to barracks and they accepted the election decision. Ozal's success in this, and the 1987 elections, was paralleled by continuing economic and societal change, dangerous internal security challenges, and momentous historical changes in global geopolitics. Assessments of how Turkey would act in a new environment were often flawed by a lack of understanding of the internal dynamics of Turkey, as discussed above, and sometimes by a dismissal of its previous consistent position on many international issues, the subject of the next chapter.

Notes

1.   Ferenc Vali, *Bridge Across the Bosporos,* ch. 2 (Baltimore and London: Johns Hopkins University Press, 1971), 43-48, gives a useful geographical tour of Turkey.

2.   Erik J. Zurcher, *Turkey, A Modern History* (London and New York: I.B. Taurus, 1993), 170-172.

3.   Kurdish people are divided between Turkey, Iran, Iraq and Syria, which creates complicated security problems for Turkey. They are a majority in much of Southeast Turkey, and assimilated in large numbers throughout the Republic. Total numbers are unknown, but are thought to comprise 10 to 15 percent of the Turkish population. Those in the tribal areas have never been comfortable under the Kemalist centralized state administration, and there were revolts in 1925, 1930, and 1937.

4.   The Alewites are Shia Muslims, comprising about a quarter of both Turks and Kurds. They have always been leading supporters of the Kemalist secular state, and they are antagonistic to orthodox Sunni Islam, as represented by Islamist parties.

5.   Arnold J. Toynbee, *A Study of History*, abridgement of vols. XVII-XX (New York: 1956), 239.

6.   Jacob Burckhardt, *On History and Historians* (New York, 1958), 213.

7.   R.N. Berki, *State and Society: An Antithesis of Modern Political Thought*, in *State and Society in Contemporary Europe*, eds. Jack Hayward and R.N. Berki (Oxford: Martin Robertson, 1979), 2-4.

8. Serif Mardin, *Ataturk: Founder of a Modern State* (London: C. Hurst, 1981), 208-209.

9. Ataturk attempted to move to a two-party system in 1930 by creating an opposition from members of the CHP. This experiment was unsuccessful and it was not revived until 1946, under Ataturk's successor President Ismet Inonu.

10. A great deal has been written on Kemalism or Ataturkism. A full description of the "Six Arrows," their interpretation, and implications is in Stanford J. Shaw and Ezel Kural Shaw, *History of the Ottoman Empire and Modern Turkey* , 2 vols. (Gateshead, Cambridge: University Press, 1977; reprinted 1994), 375-395.

11. Halil Inalcik, "Turkey between Europe and the Middle East," *Foreign Policy* 7 (1980), 7.

12. Metin Tamkoc, *The Warrior Diplomats* (Salt Lake City: University of Utah Press, 1976), 103-111. Tamkoc's book deals extensively with the characters of the first six presidents of Turkey, demonstrating how they reserved to themselves foreign policy decisions, and how the political culture of Turkey reinforced this tendency.

13. Metin Heper, *The State Tradition in Turkey* (Hul: Eothen Press, 1985), 64. This book gives an extremely interesting and credible insight into the enduring nature of the division between state and politics in Turkey, and the unique position of the Turkish military in the democratic process.

14. Heper, *State Tradition*, 45.

15. Andrew Mango, "The State of Turkey," *Middle Eastern Studies*, 13 (1977), 265.

16. In this he was given crucial help by Fevzi Cakmak, who held the post of Chief of TGS for nearly 23 years. William Hale, *Turkish Politics and the Military* (London and New York: Routledge, 1994), 70.

17. See Heper, *State Tradition*, 53, and Hale, *Military*, 81.

18. Mehmet Ali Birand, *Shirts of Steel, An Anatomy of the Turkish Armed Forces* (London and New York: I.B. Tauris, 1991), is particularly good at describing the philosophy and culture of the Turkish military. It provides a keen insight into how Turkey's armed forces, particularly the 35,000 strong officer corps, view Ataturk, the state, the military, politics, and civilians.

19. Quoted in Birand, *Shirts of Steel*, 196.

20. Quoted in Heper, *State Tradition*, 83.

21. Ibid., 96.

22. C.H. Dodd, *The Crisis of Turkish Democracy*, 2nd ed. (Oundle: Eothen Press, 1983, 26.

23. In Frederick Frey, *Patterns of Elite politics in Turkey*, quoted in Heper, *State Tradition*, 90.

24. Frank Tachau, *Turkey: The Politics of Authority, Democracy, and Development* (New York: Praeger, 1985).

25. Quoted in Heper, *State Tradition*, 131.

26. Ibid., 132.

27. Ibid., 126, taken from Article 118 of the 1982 Constitution.

28. The preamble to the 1982 Constitution states a "determination to safeguard . . . the Republic of Turkey, and to ensure it attains the standards of contemporary civilization. The determination that no protection shall be afforded to thoughts or opinions contrary to Turkish national interests, the principle of the existence of Turkey as an indivisible entity, . . and that as required by the principle of secularism, there shall be no interference whatsoever of sacred religious feelings in state affairs and politics." Dodd, *Crisis of Turkish Democracy*, 154-155.

4.

The Exercise of Turkish Foreign Policy: Ataturk to Ozal

Churchill said of the Soviet Union, "I cannot forecast for you the action of Russia. It is a riddle, wrapped in a mystery, inside an enigma." The most perceptive part of this statement, and the most often neglected, was his coda, "but perhaps there is a key. That key is Russian national interest."[1] Ataturk's Turkey had an equally focused foreign policy, intimately tied to the national mission of achieving the level of contemporary civilization, and the parallel goals of security and modernization. Like the Ottomans, he drew a distinction between the core policy and the day-to-day pursuit of this policy, He also recognized the small power status of the Republic and the need for an international aspect to the national security policy. Turkey's permanent policy was one of alignment with the West, while the temporary policy was made up of any actions required to sustain national security. Like Soviet Russia and Nazi Germany, outside observers found it difficult to evaluate the new Turkish Republic or interpret its actions objectively. However, the key to Turkey's actions could be found, set out quite unambiguously, in the National Pact, and in Ataturk's public announcements. The security imperatives of Turkey were clear, concise, and a good deal more benign than those of the majority of new postwar states.

From 1923, other than a determination to revise details of the Lausanne Treaty, the policy rejected expansion and aggression. It specifically eschewed any romantic notions of re-establishing the Ottoman Empire, and it actively suppressed pan-Turkic aspirations. It was fundamentally defensive. What was seen by the outside world would be the temporary policies required to maneuver in a dangerous environment, the whole object of which was defense of the national mission, which could be dubbed "the inverse-ghazi theory of foreign policy." Under the Ottomans the key elements in maintaining the Sultan's authority and legitimacy were martial success, territorial acquisition, and the distribution of wealth to supporters. By 1918 empire, war and alliances had all ended in catastrophe. After 1923, Ataturk based the legitimacy of the Republic on the defense of a strictly defined status quo, in which national security was paramount.

Foreign Policy Imperatives

In 1927 Ataturk addressed the GNA over a period of 6 days, setting out the history, background, and achievements of the new state, and laying down the tenets of Kemalist, and therefore Turkish, foreign policy.[2] The pursuit of national security was encapsulated in simple watchwords: "Friendship with every nation"; "Turkey has no perpetual enemies"; and most significantly, "Peace at home, peace in the world."[3] In addition he stated "the State should pursue an *exclusively national policy*. . . . When I speak of national policy I mean it in this sense: to work *within our national boundaries* for the real happiness and welfare of our nation and country by, above all, *relying on our own strength* in order to retain our existence" [emphasis added].[4]

He was equally unambiguous about his assumptions of "full sovereignty," stating: "We refer to full sovereignty as . . . complete independence and freedom of action in political, economic, judicial, military, and cultural fields. Lack of sovereignty in any one of these connotes . . . a total lack of sovereignty of nation and country."[5] Strict interpretation of these statements would be used by nationalist hardliners in the post-Ataturk era to denounce NATO membership, foreign aid,

U.S. troop-basing, and applications to join the European Community. A similar interpretation fed the demands for autarky and state control of the economy, useful in the early years of the Republic, but increasingly economically self-defeating in the late 20th century.

This self-centered policy had its drawbacks. It encouraged introspection and ethnocentricity. It fostered a mindset that could view the world only from a Turkish perspective. To the Turks their break with the Ottoman legacy, and their disavowal of territorial ambition, made the continuing antagonism of neighbors frustrating and angering. Turks saw conspiracies and threats everywhere, both to their external security, and to the unity and integrity of the state. This attitude had justification but ignored the fact that other countries too had legitimate concerns. Turkey was, and is, a lone wolf. Until the collapse of the Soviet Union released the Turkic Republics of the Trans-Caucasus and Central Asia, Turkey had no natural or instinctive friends or allies. The reality of Turkey's position and its perception of the outside world neatly fitted the old aphorism, "just because you are paranoid, doesn't mean they are not after you."

International Acceptance

What Ataturk set out was a status quo, nationalist, and neutralist foreign policy. It was to be driven by the same secular, political imperatives as those of the foreign policies of the West. He had no ethnic pan-Turkic ambitions, no Islamic brotherhood romanticism, and no political internationalist aspirations. However, not only was Turkey faced with the antagonism of neighboring states but there were deep and real European misgivings about the re-emergence of the "Turk" as a power in the region. Ataturk recognized the strength of these antipathies, and also the environment within which he was attempting to consolidate the state. Turkey was weak, exhausted, under-resourced, and distrusted. The key to recovery and development was peace, and peace would be achieved by basing security policy on four pillars: the declared renunciation of aggressive, expansionist intent; the strongest possible defense of territorial integrity through the maintenance of a strong army; international acceptance, particularly by the West; and regional security arrangements.

It was at this stage that Ataturk was helped most by the goodwill of the new Soviet Union. In the 1920s both states were international outcasts, wracked by problems of revolutionary transformation. In 1925 the Treaty of Friendship and Neutrality confirmed the agreement of 1921. In 1926 Turkey reached an accommodation with Britain over the Mosul region of Iraq and the Kirkut oilfields.[6] In 1930 Ataturk and the formidable Greek Prime Minister, Venizelos, concluded a Turco-Greek treaty, overcoming historical hatred, the experiences of the most recent war, and the distaste of both publics. Ataturk clearly identified the strategic unity of the Aegean and the damage in institutionalizing Turkish-Greek enmity. His authority gave him the ability to dismiss domestic misgivings and Turkish-Greek relations would remain correct, if not warm, until the 1960s. In 1932 Ataturk took Turkey into the League of Nations, effectively ending its isolation and re-affirming the traditional Ottoman desire for international acceptance within a formal, legal framework.

Ataturk foresaw that the days of empire were numbered. From 1921 he had said "Let us recognize our own limits" and "Turkey does not desire an inch of foreign territory, but it will not give up an inch of what it holds."[7] Domestic development was not fast enough to shape Turkey in the democratic image of the West but, in return for recognition and respect for Turkey's territorial integrity, Ataturk offered the West a zone of stability in a volatile area. This has remained a consistent theme to the present day. For Turks, the advantages to the West of their responsible, conservative foreign policy in this vitally important area was never sufficiently recognized.

Turkey could not remain immune from global developments. Ataturk's priorities did not change, but the temporary policy had to be responsive to political reality. In 1934, in conversation with General Douglas MacArthur, he predicted with uncanny precision the course of international affairs that would lead again to world war.[8] Ataturk moved to place Turkey in the best position to face the approaching upheaval. He did not feel Turkey was threatened directly for its own sake, but he foresaw the difficulty of staying aloof from the conflict. The options were all poor. The Western democracies were weak and unprepared, a natural Turkish affinity to Germany was negated by the ideological poison of Nazism, and a full alliance with Russia was out of the question. Turkey had nothing to gain from a war that threatened the unconsolidated foundations of the new Republic. In a burst of what has been described as "pactomania," Ataturk sought to create a degree of regional stability. In 1934 he concluded a Balkan Pact, and in 1937 he settled relations in the East with the Saadabad Pact. Neither of these could be considered more than weak nonaggression treaties and pious expressions of goodwill, but they had significance in giving Turkey a reputation for regional leadership, and further advertising the pacific intentions of the Republic.

Of greater significance was the 1936 Montreux Convention, which returned full control of the Straits to Turkey. Once again Ataturk submitted his claims with full legal justification. This contrasted with the Germans, who unilaterally reoccupied the Rhinelands, and with the Italians, who invaded Abyssinia. Turkey's claims were accepted by the Lausanne signatories.[9] In 1939 Turkey at last achieved the final revision of the Lausanne Treaty, when France ceded to Turkey the Syrian province of Hatay. Ataturk did not live to see this, having died in November 1938, handing uncontested power on to his close military and political colleague, Ismet Inonu.

Turkey and the Second World War

The record of Turkey's involvement in World War Two is covered quickly, but it illustrates the consistent fundamentals of Turkish security policy, even in a dramatically changed international environment.[10] Inonu, even more than Ataturk, represented the conservative, cautious aspect of Turkish policy. Despite intense pressure from both sides in the conflict, Turkey contrived to stay neutral until the closing months of the war. Despite later criticism, particularly from the Russians, this stance was neither craven nor cynical. There is no doubt that both official and majority Turkish opinion was firm in desiring an allied victory, but Turkey had to accept the realities of its geographical and political position, its weak economy, and its antiquated armed forces. Germany at first attempted to play on 19th century and First World War sentiment. Later, after its successes in Russia and North Africa, it tried to tempt Turkey into the war with pan-Turkic prospects in Central Asia and the Trans-Caucasus.[11] Mindful of Ataturk's warning against "grandiose dreams that are not in our power to achieve,"[12] Inonu communicated to Hitler that "Turkey had enough to do in fully developing its own territory, and had not the slightest interest in any acquisition of territory."[13] Conversely, in the face of German fears that Turkey may openly side with the Allies, even allowing Russian bases, he said "I told that obstinate Lord Curzon (at Lausanne) that every Turk would stake his life rather than again make concessions to a foreign power, and this view is more deeply ingrained than ever in my people in their political maturity."[14]

However, by 1943, as the German potential to invade Turkey was removed, Inonu was able to maneuver Turkey closer and closer to the Allies. It was obvious that the Allies would drive the new postwar agenda, and Turkey needed to be in a position to benefit from this. On 23 February 1945 Turkey declared war on Germany, thereby ensuring itself a seat in the new U.N. organization.

Turkey Moves West

By late 1944 Turkey was already concerned about two issues of critical importance to itself: the role of the Straits in the postwar world, and the role of the Balkans and the Northern

Tier (Greece, Turkey, Iran) in the new power alignments. This reflected traditional worries, now overlain by the global ideological divide between America, with no natural inclination toward Turkey, and Russia, the historical enemy. The Soviets moved fast to bring Turkey back into the center stage of great power rivalry by renouncing the 1925 treaty. They wanted a new agreement that reflected the new regional and global situation more accurately. Turkey was not in a strong position to refuse, but at this stage the Russians grossly overplayed their hand. Russia was already signaling its intentions in Iran, Greece, and across Eastern Europe when they announced the price of renewed Russo-Turkish accord: the retrocession of two provinces of Eastern Turkey, establishment of Soviet bases in the Straits, and revision of the Montreux Convention. The Soviets coyly implied that a complete reorientation of Turkish foreign policy would obviate the need for these specific demands. The West saw clearly that the Soviet intention was not merely to gain control of a vital waterway, but also to induce a change in Turkey's internal regime with the aim of ending its Western orientation.

Crises in all the northern tier countries forced the United States to reformulate its policy in an area in which it had previously had little interest. In July 1946, in the wake of Churchill's "Iron Curtain" speech at Fulton, Missouri, the USS *Missouri* made a port visit to Istanbul.[15] An American memorandum of October 1946 described Turkey as the most important strategic factor in the Eastern Mediterranean and the Middle East. It also noted that it was a broadly united country, firm in its opposition to Russia, but that its military requirements were becoming a dangerous drain on the economy. It recommended that Turkey be given economic and military support.[16]

In March 1947 Truman put to the Senate and House a bill for a $400 million appropriation to aid Greece and Turkey. This was the first significant action in what became known as the Truman Doctrine, and it would have profound effects on how the United States, and consequently its allies, would conduct relations with Russia and other Communist states. In specific terms it anchored Turkey firmly in the Western camp, well beyond the broad ideological orientation of the early years of the Republic.

Turkey and the Cold War

Soviet actions clearly constituted a mortal threat to Turkey's integrity and demanded a commitment to the West beyond ideology. Without this, it is conceivable Turkey may have adhered to a neutralist policy, seeking friendly relations in every direction. Full participation in the complicated, developing political, military, and economic system of Atlantic and European integration would now safeguard its national security.

Despite recognition of Turkey's importance, and the commitments of the Truman Doctrine, the Western powers were reluctant to extend the relationship formally. Turkey gained admission to the Council of Europe and the Organization for European Economic Co-operation, but the debate over its membership of the all important North Atlantic Treaty Organization (NATO) highlighted again the ambivalence of the West to Turkey's credentials as a "European" country. In discussions that would reflect similar debates at the close of the Cold War, America and its European allies were reluctant to be drawn into binding security guarantees with a country bordering the volatile Middle East. As the 1990 Gulf War gave Ozal a golden opportunity to demonstrate Turkey's continuing importance, so the 1950 Korean War gave the new DP government the chance to demonstrate its solidarity with the West, the United Nations, and particularly with NATO's strongest member, the United States.

In 1952, Turkey, along with Greece, acceded to NATO.[17] In 1953 it concluded a Balkan Defense Treaty with Greece and Yugoslavia, and in 1955 the Baghdad Pact with Britain, Iraq, Pakistan and Iran, although not America. In 1958, with the defection of Iraq, this was renamed the Central Treaty

44

Organization (CENTO). Coming in parallel with Turkish moves to multiparty democracy, the period of the 1950s was a golden age in Turkey's relations with the West. Its responsible, prudent foreign policy, combined with its demonstrable allegiance to Western political institutions, brought Turkey security, significant military assistance, international acceptance, entry to the coveted Western "clubs," foreign aid, and economic support. Relations with the United States, in particular, were intensified to an extraordinary degree.

In many ways it was too good to last. Foreign policy had always been national policy, and the stature of Ataturk and Inonu ensured that official policy represented the unanimous will of the nation. Given Turkey's obsession with national integrity and security, a one-party state facing an obvious threat had little difficulty in formulating foreign policy. However the relaxing of the Soviet threat after Stalin's death, economic mismanagement, and the increasingly volatile nature of domestic politics drew foreign policy into the domestic arena. In 1960 the military intervened to depose the Menderes government.[18] Officially the foreign policy line of Turkey remained unchanged, and the military leaders issued the following message:

> We are addressing ourselves to our Allies, friends, neighbors, and the entire world: Our aim is to remain completely loyal to the UN Charter and to the principles of human rights; the principle of peace at home and in the world set by the great Ataturk is our flag. We are loyal to all our alliances and undertakings. We believe in NATO and CENTO and we are faithful to them.[19]

The 1960 revolution opened a new era in domestic politics, and out of this political upheaval the changing character of the Turkish nation-state, and a dynamic international scene, could not fail to affect Turkish foreign policy.

Turkey Reassesses its Role

Samuel Johnson said, "The fatal disease of friendship is gradual decay, or dislike, hourly increased by causes too slender for complaint and too numerous for removal."[20] Undoubtedly the more liberal press laws of 1961 allowed outlets for the small, but vocal opponents of Turkey's foreign policy orientation. These included the pro-Islamists with their desire for closer relations with Muslim countries, the ultranationalists demanding the full sovereignty set out by Ataturk, and leftists, drawn politically to communism, or economically to a command economy. Governments had to acknowledge these groups, particularly when they portrayed themselves as more Ataturkist than the government. However, as noted in the last chapter, a change of government in itself had little impact on the orientation of foreign policy. A civil servant likened national security objectives and governments to a watch and the wearer; it didn't matter whose wrist it was on, it would still tell the same time.[21] Therefore the debates looked noisy to the outside world, but the hold of the state over issues of national security was hardly loosened. External events continued to have far greater effect on foreign policy decisions than the oscillations of domestic politics. What was important were the changes of attitude that took place within the elite.

There had been a wedge driven into the Turco-American relationship during the Cuban missile crisis, but the catalyst for a major reassessment of the relationship came in 1964 with the growing tension in Cyprus and mounting violence by the Greek Cypriots against the Turkish minority. For the first time public opinion was brought to bear on a foreign policy issue. In this situation the Turks considered military intervention. In response, President Johnson wrote expressing "grave concern" and significantly adding "NATO Allies have not had a chance to consider whether they have an obligation to protect Turkey against the Soviet Union if Turkey takes a step which results in Soviet intervention." In addition he spelt out the bilateral agreement whereby Turkey agreed not to use "military assistance for purposes other than those for which such assistance was furnished."[22] It was to be the first of a number of such limitations on the use of foreign supplied equipment for anything other than defense against external aggression.

The effect of Johnson's letter cannot be overstated. It severely unsettled the government, the MFA, and the military. It heightened a Turkish sense of insecurity by calling into question their assumption of support from an organization they had loyally supported. It highlighted their dependency on the Americans and exposed to them how internationally isolated they were if their security concerns did not coincide totally with those of the West.[23] When the Johnson letter itself went public in 1966, presumably with official blessing, it played to all the traditional fears of exclusion from the European-Christian club and excited violent anti-American feelings. From this time the Turkish public began to "weigh a nation's friendship or animosity to Turkey by its stand on the Cyprus issue."[24] This animosity was fueled by Turkey's intense sensitivity over sovereignty, unavoidable cultural differences, a realization of growing dependency that bore comparison to the "capitulations," and a damaged image of America during the Vietnam War. The Turkish Government used the leak of the Johnson letter to renegotiate the complete range of formal and informal bilateral agreements, bringing them together under a single Co-operation Agreement Concerning Joint Defense in 1969.[25] This was further rationalized under the Defense and Economic Co-operation Agreement (DECA) of 1980.

This had all taken place during a period when counter-productive Soviet antagonism had shifted to peaceful, if wary, co-existence. Turkey looked around to find that its image of a faithful, servile follower of the West had led to the West taking it for granted and other states dismissing it as an agent of Western "imperialism." In this spirit Turkey attempted to reduce further its tensions with Russia and to re-establish its Islamic credentials through the Third World, particularly in the Middle East.

The latter change in policy was always burdened by paradoxes. The rapprochement with Arab Muslims began before the OPEC oil embargo of 1973, so could not be called hypocritical. But, although closer relations with Islamic states reflected the inclination of the conservative, rural majority of Turkey, the ethnic, historical and geopolitical divisions proved stronger than any common religious heritage. The Republic's secular nature, Western orientation, anti-Communist tradition, pro-Israeli stance, and traditional antipathy to adventurism severely constrained any active or dynamic policy and undermined a leadership role. Any potential leadership role was in its turn resisted by Russia, the Arab League, and Iran, all with a vested interest in limiting Turkey's influence in the region. Despite this, Turkey sought rapprochement with Muslim countries, joining the Organization of Islamic Conference (OIC) in 1976. In 1977 Iraq began building its oil pipeline from Kirkut to Iskenderum.[26]

The Coup by Memorandum of 1971 had had no effect on foreign policy, but Turkish intervention in Cyprus in 1974 was a definite departure from Turkey's traditionally conservative approach and greatly complicated external relations for itself and for its allies. Turkey's actions in Cyprus were used by Turkey's enemies and critics as evidence of the continuing aggressive and expansionist nature of the "Turk." Examination of Turkey's security policy and the facts of the Cyprus episode do not bear this out. Turkey strove hard to get the international community to stand by its responsibilities, but failed. It had never made a claim to Cyprus but justified its actions on the grounds of defense of the Turkish Cypriot minority and a clear breach, by the Greeks, of the London Treaty, which had established an independent Cyprus. The cool but workable Turco-Greek relations established in 1930 had been damaged severely by the 1964 Cyprus crisis, but they were now shattered by the events of 1974. Despite the obvious advantages that lay in avoiding confrontation, Cyprus was a catalyst for opening a Pandora's Box of bilateral issues over which to disagree. These included borders, ethnic minorities, the Aegean islands, oil exploration, territorial seas, and airspace limitations. In 1963 Turkey had signed the Ankara Agreement, which set out an agenda and program whereby Turkey could eventually accede to the then European Community. This issue would carry its own problems and issues, but in the meantime, Greece, which was already a member, used this as another stick to beat Turkey.[27] The 1974 disturbance exacerbated every one of these issues and brought Turkey under the scrutiny of Western public opinion. Despite the acknowledged importance of its strategic position, and its consistently conservative foreign policy, Turkey found its actions in Cyprus provided an issue around which its enemies, notably orchestrated by the Greek and Armenian Diaspora, could mobilize. In this process they garnered a broad spectrum of opinion, critical of authoritarian regimes in general and focusing on Turkey's human rights and democratic track record in particular. The weight of this opinion in America led the U.S. Congress to suspend all military aid and weapons sales to Turkey until 1979.

It was at this stage that the luxury of mutual recriminations became inappropriate and dangerous. In early 1979 the Shah's regime in Iran collapsed, and in December the Russians invaded Afghanistan, opening the "second Cold War." In 1980 Iraq invaded Iran. The northern tier looked fragile again, and Turkey looked indispensable. However, these dramatic external events coincided with the rising political polarization and violence within Turkey. Although America concluded the DECA Agreement, and commentators announced that Turkey's "flirtation with Russia and the nonaligned world . . .[and] multi-dimensional diplomacy. . . had been abandoned,"[28] the American administration doubted if Turkey could play the regional role assigned to it, under the existing government. Against this background the military intervened in September 1980.

Security Policy Stability

Under the military regime, foreign policy came back unequivocally into the domain of the military, whose external priorities reflected their obsession with national security, and therefore demanded an alignment with the West on a par with that of the 1950s. In many ways, the period of the early to mid-1980s suited Turkey's foreign policy makers well. The certainties of the Cold War remained, placing comforting limitations on its own actions, and useful ones on those of its neighbors, including Greece. Deep worries over the Russian invasion of Afghanistan were replaced by a realization that Russia had committed itself to a debilitating, unwinnable war, further reducing a direct Soviet threat to Turkey. A confident America under President Reagan redefined the Cold War in moral, ideological terms, while daring Russia to match it in a new high technology arms race. As part of this, the American financial and arms commitment to Turkey had been restored, although the politics of the Southern Region required a return to the evenhandedness of the Truman era, and Greece and Turkey now received aid at a 7:10 ratio. The acrimony over the deployment of Pershing 2 and Cruise missiles was buried, and NATO confidence returned, based on a restored belief that détente with the Soviets was better pursued from a position of strength. Turkey's position within this key institution remained important. The Iran-Iraq War ground on, but the worrying prospect of an outright victory for either side receded. Two regional competitors were weakening themselves, and Turkey had the opportunity to benefit from trade with both. On the basis of restored domestic and external stability, the military opted to return to barracks, accepting the 1983 election victory of Turgut Ozal's Motherland party.

Notes

1. Winston Churchill, *Modern Quotations* (London: Penguin Books, 1980), 73:2.

2. Kemal Ataturk, speech delivered by Ghazi Mustapha Kemal, President of the Turkish Republic, October 1927 (Leipzig: K. F. Koehler, 1929).

3. Lord Kinross, *Ataturk: The Rebirth of a Nation* (London: Weidenfeld and Nicholson, 1993), 458.

4. Ataturk, *A Speech,* 242.

5. Turkkaya Ataov, *Turkish Foreign Policy 1939-1945* (Ankara: Faculty of Political Sciences of the University of Ankara, 1965), 1.

6. The Turkish claim to Mosul was debatable on ethnic grounds, but it was part of the National Pact. The British government certainly knew of the potential of the Kirkut oil fields, but Ataturk was unwilling to jeopardize Turkey's broader relationship with the West over this matter. Mosul went to Iraq.

7. Kinross, *Ataturk,* 458.

8. Ibid., 463.

9. Full accounts of the complexity of the Montreux Convention are in Ferenc Vali, *Bridge Across the Bosporos,* ch. 2 (Baltimore and London: Johns Hopkins University Press, 1971), 187-190, and Ferenc A. Vali, *The Turkish Straits and NATO* (Stanford: Hoover Institution Studies, 1972), 40-57.

10. Full accounts of Turkey's foreign policy in World War Two are in Ataov, *Turkish Foreign Policy 1939-1945,* and Edward Weisband, *Turkish Foreign Policy 1939-1945, Small State Diplomacy and Great Power Reality* (Princeton: Princeton University Press, 1973).

11. The Turkish foreign minister's reply to this generous German offer was "I must have Scotland as well." Ataov, *Turkish Foreign Policy,* 101.

12. Ibid., 97.

13. Ibid.

14. Ibid., 99.

15. In his enthusiasm the mayor of Istanbul opened the city's brothels to the U.S. sailors for free, an event that is still remembered with a little embarrassment in Turkey.

16. Bruce R. Kuniholm, *The Origins of the Cold War in the Near East, Great Power Conflict and Diplomacy in Iran, Turkey, and Greece* (Princeton: Princeton University Press, 1980), 375. At this

point Turkey was maintaining a fully mobilized army of 500,000, at a cost of 38 percent of the national budget.

17. Territorial definitions in the original Washington Treaty had to be altered to accept Turkey's membership.

18. How deeply the Democratic Party government alienated the "elite" can be gauged by the fact that the army put President Bayar under sentence of death, and executed Prime Minister Menderes and the Foreign Minister.

19. Vali, *Bridge,* 40.

20. Samuel Johnson, quoted in Nuri Even, "Turkey, NATO, and Europe—a Deteriorating Relationship," *Atlantic Papers* 34, December 1977, 54.

21. Heper, *State Tradition,* 82.

22. Quoted in Vali, *Bridge,* 130.

23. In a 1965 opinion poll the question "who is our best friend?" gave the United States 18 percent, Germany 24 percent, and "we have none" 25 percent. America even achieved 8 percent as "the greatest enemy", although Greece and Russia topped this section with 42 percent and 34 percent respectively. America's role in international affairs attracted 66 percent negative reactions, however Turkey's membership of NATO was endorsed by 78 percent. Not overmuch should be read into these figures but they illustrate the ambivalence in Turkey's officially declared attachment to the West (Vali, *Bridge,* 107-112).

24. Metin Toker, *Milliyet* ,11 October 1967, cited in Metin Tamkoc, *The Warrior Diplomats* (Salt Lake City: University of Utah Press, 1976), 284.

25. Turkey and the United States had entered into some 55 bi-lateral agreements of various binding natures. The sensitivity of some of these arrangements to the government, MFA, and military was such that many were not even put to the GNA.

26. Philip Robins, *Turkey and the Middle East* (London: Chatham House Papers, 1991), 114-117.

27. Full details of Turco-Greek bi-lateral issues, too much to cover in this paper, are in Suha Bolukbasi, *The Turco-Greek Dispute,* in, Dodd, ed, *Turkish Foreign Policy,* 27-54. It is a Turkish account but objective.

28. "Reoccidentation," *The Economist,* 5 April 1980.

5.
The Mold Breaks

Between 1989 and 1992 the global geopolitical mold broke. There were encouraging signs of reduced East-West tension under Gorbachev, but few saw this new détente as presaging the complete collapse of the Cold War structure. In November 1989 the Berlin Wall fell, leading to the unification of Germany the following year. In August 1990 Iraq invaded Kuwait, and the real end of the Cold War was marked by Russian support for U.S.-sponsored U.N. resolutions against a former Soviet client-state. In December 1991 the Soviet Union itself was dissolved, and a new hybrid, the Commonwealth of Independent States (CIS) appeared.

A revolution in world affairs had taken place, less sanguinary than the revolutions of 1918 and 1945, but equally significant. The implications for Turkish foreign policy makers were dramatic, challenging, and worrying. At a stroke, the strategic center of gravity moved from Germany to Turkey, but the extinction of the East-West axis of confrontation almost immediately put Turkey into the neglected category again. The conventional view that judged strategic importance in the context of the Cold War was initially apt to discount Turkey in the new calculations. Yet few states were more directly affected by the collapse of the Soviet Union, and almost no state had such direct and diverse interests in the new environment, than Turkey.

Suddenly, the whole area of Turkey's historical ethnic roots opened up, with the emergence of independent states in the Trans-Caucasus and Central Asia. The whole area of former Ottoman domination was open, as both Middle Eastern and

53

Balkan politics were lifted from the context of superpower confrontation. In Turkey, Islamists and pan-Turkists discovered new Muslim and Turkic states, communities, and minorities that appeared to demand a lead from Turkey. Suppressed for nearly 70 years, these enthusiasms encompassed the new Turkic states of Azerbaijan, Turkmenistan, Uzbekistan, Kazakhstan, and Kirghizstan, and also such historically esoteric groups as Uighur Chinese, the Tartars and Chechens of Russia, Abkhazians from Georgia, the Moldovan Gagauz, and Bosnian Muslims.[1]

The Challenge

The Chinese have no single character for the word "crisis." It consists of a diagram that conveys the twin concepts of "danger" and "opportunity." By this definition, the increasingly benign global environment from 1985 on rapidly began to constitute a "crisis" for the cautious, conservative Kemalist elite. Turkey faced the reality of being at the epicenter of a volatile region, without constraints, where local animosities and ambitions readily flared into war. To the south, Saddam Hussein, the Iraqi leader, having at last concluded his 8-year conflict with Iran, was turning his eyes to the oil-rich state of Kuwait. To the northeast, the ethnically Armenian province of Nagorno-Karabakh was attempting to secede from Turkic Azerbaijan. To the northwest, the artificial state of Yugoslavia was beginning to splinter under the pressures of nationalism and Serbian aggression.

The new situation clearly demanded imaginative responses to a range of new challenges, but the excitement of the popular press, and the prospect of an enhanced regional role were viewed with caution by the MFA and military, who sought to adhere to a traditional policy. Intervention in Cyprus had led to a costly, long-term commitment that had caused constant friction in both domestic and foreign affairs, and the state elite were very wary of unilateral action, or anything that smacked of adventurism. It is against this background that the significance of Turgut Ozal, as Prime Minister, and subsequently President, must be viewed.

Turgut Ozal

Opinion in Turkey is still divided on whether Ozal was a dangerous adventurist or a visionary, committed to moving Turkey from a transcendentalist to an instrumentalist state, while re-orientating Turkey's foreign policy to meet the challenges of the post-Cold War era. What is not in doubt is that from 1983 to his death in 1993, Ozal was the most dominant figure in Turkish politics since Inonu, and the most radical since Ataturk himself. He was by nature a controversial figure. Half Kurdish, he had also been a member of the banned National Salvation Party, forerunner of the Refah Party. Ozal was an engineer and an economic technocrat. He served on the Turkish State Planning Organization and with the World Bank. In 1979 he had been undersecretary to Prime Minister Demirel, and he was retained by General Evren to be Deputy Prime Minister responsible for economic affairs after the 1980 Coup.

From his election success in 1983, Ozal set about re-ordering the main tenets of Turkish security policy. He wanted to use the new environment to break from the stifling obsession with territorial security, which perpetuated the dominance of state over society, and base national security and a strong regional role on successful economic development. Because of the continuing dominance of the military both in external and internal affairs, this development was slow, but it gathered momentum after Ozal's election success of 1987. The cumulative effects of introducing free-market economics, privatization, export-promotion, a fully convertible currency, and a development philosophy of "build, operate, transfer"[2] were dramatic and had important political and social consequences. Ozal understood that a country's economic strength is universally recognized as the single most important indicator of the power and capability to support a state's foreign policy objectives. On this basis independent military

55

power is only a function of the economic vitality and the underlying industrial-technological sophistication of a country.[3] U.S. support for the Turkish military had disguised this. Ozal saw that in the New World Order a nation's strategic importance would be increasingly measured by its economic viability and prowess. From the 1940s Ataturk's mission to "raise Turkey to the level of contemporary civilisation" had always been undermined by a bald assumption that strength was synonymous with military force and autarky. Given Turkey's traditional interest in Japan's status in the world, Ozal's reforms belatedly acknowledged why Japan, a military dwarf, sat firmly among the advanced nations, while Turkey was only seen as important in security terms.

There are those who claim that Ozal anticipated the collapse of the Soviet Union well ahead of the traditionally cautious military and MFA.[4] While continuing to disclaim any Turkish territorial ambitions, Ozal thought that circumstances would soon allow Turkey to reposition itself and to project its interests into the three regions of which it was part. Ozal also anticipated the enhanced position of the United States as the sole remaining superpower, whose new global strategy would require the support of regional allies. Turkey's critical geostrategic position made it ideally suited to be one of those allies, and to benefit from offering that support. The EU was important to Ozal for the major export market it represented,[5] and he shared with the Turkish elite the symbolic importance of joining the premier politico-economic European "club." In 1987 he submitted an application for full membership.[6] He was aware of the strict economic criteria for membership (soon to be strengthened under the 1992 Maastricht Agreement), and while he may have had no real expectation of early acceptance, he raised domestic expectations that were to lead to disappointment and frustration.[7]

Whatever Ozal's intentions, until 1990 Turkish foreign policy was dynamic but not yet revolutionary. If one accepts the fundamental consistency of Turkish security policy, it represented another chapter in the requirement of Turkey's "permanent" policy to adapt its "temporary" policy to changing global and regional conditions. It took into account national security, territorial integrity, and regional arrangements, while maintaining an orientation to the West. At the same time it recognized the opportunity for an increasingly broad-based national foreign policy harking back to Turkey's pre-Cold War regional role. The important difference was Ozal's recognition of the need to adjust Turkey's domestic political, social, and economic arrangements if Turkey was to be able to profit from new opportunities.

The Gulf War

In October 1989 Ozal was elected President, while ANAP remained in power. In December, Mesut Yilmaz, the foreign minister, convened a meeting of Turkey's European ambassadors to assess Turkey's foreign policy after the fall of the Berlin Wall. The meeting concluded that Turkey's interests were best served by remaining in NATO; closer ties with Russia, East Europe and the former Soviet Republics must be formed; and in the future, security threats would come primarily from the South (Iraq or Syria) and the West (Greece). Overall, Turkey's strategic value to the West was reduced but by no means eliminated.[8]

The Iraqi invasion of Kuwait on 2 August 1990 was a heaven-sent opportunity for Ozal. He had identified the international trends but there had been little chance to capitalize on them. Although he was to be accused of subordinating Turkey's foreign policy to the United States, his decision to whole-heartedly support the coalition was both visionary and pragmatic. The decision to cut the Kirkut-Yurmurtalik pipeline on 6 August 1990 indicated an unequivocal choice to put all of Turkey's weight on the side of the Western alliance. In this he was encouraged to expect significant compensation at the successful conclusion of the crisis, while he used Saddam's aggression as the opportunity to confront one of Turkey's most serious potential security problems.[9]

In the West these actions were seen as the natural response of a NATO ally with its own strong regional interests, and support for the United Nations in confronting aggression. In fact, much of the Turkish political establishment opposed both the substance and the style of Ozal's policies. In drawing Turkey into Middle Eastern affairs, Ozal was breaking, or at least setting aside, key assumptions of foreign policy from the National Pact onwards: noninterference in inter-Arab disputes; compartmentalization of Western policy and Middle East policy; and maintenance of correct bilateral relations with all states in the region. On 12 August 1990 Ozal sought extensive war powers from the GNA, declaring "it is impossible to pursue a hesitant policy of waiting for others to make decisions first."[10] On 2 March 1991, emboldened by the overwhelming success of the coalition, and the apparent vindication of his actions, he said, "It is my conviction that Turkey should leave its former passive and hesitant policies and engage in an active foreign policy."[11] In the course of the crisis Ozal speculated on providing troops to the coalition, opening a second front, and even seizing the Kirkut oil-fields in the event of a complete collapse of Iraqi central authority.[12] Directly or indirectly he precipitated the resignations of the Minister of Foreign Affairs, the Minister of Defense, and the Chief of TGS. His actions were criticized in the press and in the GNA, where Demirel, leader of the center-right True Path Party (DYP), spoke of "Turkish blood shed in those deserts for 400 years." Some criticism was political, some only reflected disquiet about the timing of Ozal's initiatives, but much was the result of a tradition of keeping a low profile in international affairs.

The World Unfolds

The stated Coalition aim of throwing Iraq out of Kuwait had been achieved, but no one had a clear idea of what should now determine events in Iraq itself. The West had demonized Saddam, but he had widespread popular support in the Muslim world, and few countries in the region, including Turkey, wanted to destroy the territorial integrity of Iraq. It soon became clear that only Saddam's military power could hold the country together, but the price was the brutal suppression of Kurdish and Shiite revolts. By mid-1991, a scrappy arrangement was in place. Saddam was still in Baghdad, but his actions were constrained by UN inspection teams, no-fly zones, and Operation *Provide Comfort*, which created a de facto Kurdish autonomous state on Iraq's border with Turkey. This added significant complications to Turkey's actions in its own Kurdish area.

In December 1991 the Soviet Union formally dissolved and Turkey was confronted with the requirement to address a range of new bilateral arrangements. Ozal was not the only one to be carried away by the prospects this offered to Turkey. There were enthusiasts both at home and abroad, particularly in the Bush administration. The United States, scarred by the Iranian Revolution of 1979 and confronted with rising Islamic fundamentalism in other areas of national interest, saw democratic, secular Turkey as the ideal vehicle to spearhead Western influence into the new Turkic republics. Ozal agreed. Turkey would reinforce its ethnic, religious, linguistic and historical ties, with technical, financial, and educational support; in helping these countries, Turkey would be helping itself. In addition it would be staking a claim to the massive energy potential of Central Asia and Azerbaijan. This stake would not simply be access to oil and gas, but it would also include the whole issue of pipeline development, refinement, shipment, and transit rights.

One should not be dismissive of the challenge this vision presented to Turkey, nor of the enthusiasm and ambitions that underlay the vision. Every country was now faced with the problems of new embassies, new or enlarged international fora, new legal complications, business opportunities, and the interpretation of new regional balances. Turkey appeared to have more to gain than most and seemed well placed to take advantage of new opportunities. There were also dangers. Countries also had to determine responses to new conflicts that sprang from the end of the Cold War. Turkey had a direct interest in many of them, not only from a conventional security angle, but also through parties with strong cultural, ethnic or religious ties to Turkey. Ozal had released many issues into the public domain which, combined with the growing liberalization of the press, brought increasingly outspoken public opinion to bear on government and the state.

In the face of this multifaceted challenge, Kemal Kirisci identifies two distinct categories of Turkish foreign policy activity. The first included initiatives to manage conflict in areas bordering Turkey and sought to mobilize the international community to support multilateral actions that coincided with Turkish objectives. That primary objective, as ever, was to ensure that regional conflict did not escalate to a level that threatened Turkish security. The second concentrated on long-term efforts to secure a stable international order to act as a brake on the volatile tendencies of the region.[13] This demonstrated the continuity of the "small power" approach to foreign affairs, drawing on international support, and backed by strict adherence to legalism, the rejection of the use of force to alter boundaries, and the eschewing of unilateral actions. The cases of Armenia-Azerbaijan and the Bosnia conflict illustrate the finely tuned efforts to balance domestic calls for intervention with an attempt to mobilize the international community in support of Turkish interests. The renewed primacy of this type of policy reflected the altered balance of political power in Turkey, where the DYP success in the 1991 elections brought about a new, conservative policy making coalition that undermined the dynamic aspirations of Ozal.

Armenia, Azerbaijan, and Nagorno-Karabakh

The dissolution of the Soviet Union confronted Turkey with particular problems in the Trans-Caucasus. In an area of historical competition among Turkey, Russia, and Iran, local instability gave Russia an almost immediate pretext for new involvement. Turkey was faced with Russian meddling in the

Georgian civil war and in the separatist challenge to Azerbaijan from Nagorno-Karabakh. Turkey and Armenia had been striving to reach accommodation, but the situation in Azerbaijan forced them into opposing ethnic camps. There was growing public pressure to support Azerbaijan actively, but Turkey could not contemplate war with Armenia, for fear of provoking a Russian response, while its actual ability to assist was extremely limited because it did not possess a common border. In 1992 and 1993 there were strident calls for military intervention, including statements from President Ozal himself. However, Demirel, supported by the army, made it clear that "Turkey would not act alone militarily" and argued that "foreign policy decisions cannot go along with street level excitement."[14] Instead, Turkey closed the border with Armenia and embarked on an energetic round of diplomatic activity. These actions resulted in support for the Turco-Azeri position and the acceptance of a cease-fire in the area while negotiations took place. Despite this diplomatic success for "traditional" Turkish policy, it was seen by both Turkish public opinion and international opinion as an early indication of the limitations of both Turkish ambition and influence.

The War in Bosnia

From its earliest stages Turkey was worried about growing violence in former Yugoslavia. Concern was not just for the Bosnians, but encompassed the whole Balkans with its plethora of ethnic, religious and historical connections.[15] From the start public opinion called for action, and both the Turkish Government and the West were accused of disinterest or inadequate response. Public disillusion with the West in particular became more pronounced the longer the conflict went on.

The government and the policy makers were well aware of the complexity of the issues involved and the difficulties of military intervention. Initial official response was therefore no more than active support for U.N. and NATO actions to impose sanctions on Serbia, and Turkey contributed fully to Operations *Sharp Guard* and *Deny Flight*. These sanctions further compounded the economic losses Turkey was already suffering through U.N. sanctions on Iraq, and its own embargo on Armenia. In July 1992, Demirel pulled together a pan-Turkic pressure group, this time calling for an international Gulf War-style operation in the area, and offering troops for a peace-enforcement action. While this was rejected, in 1994 Turkey at last felt it had enough support for the deployment of 1,500 troops, and a similar force joined the Implementation Force (IFOR) that supervised the 1995/96 Dayton Peace Agreement.

The lack of decisiveness by Western governments in limiting or halting the violence in Bosnia was particularly difficult for the Turkish government with a foot in both camps. In Western circles the Turks were seen as being too close to the problem, and in Muslim circles they were seen either as a cats-paw of the West, or as incapable of providing the leadership role they aspired to. In the face of this disappointment, they tried to use the OIC to mobilize support for lifting the arms embargo on the Bosnian Muslims. Failure to get U.N. support for this initiative further raised the level of domestic criticism of the government. However, despite this, Turkey refused to be drawn into unilateral actions that would not be supported by the international community. Underlying Turkish actions in both Azerbaijan and Bosnia was a secular determination not to allow these conflicts to be portrayed as ones of religion, or to "plunge Turkey into such trouble that we would be unable to disentangle ourselves for 20 years . . . it would turn the matter into a Muslim-Christian conflict."[16]

The Turkic Republics of Central Asia

It was in Central Asia that Turkey saw it might gain unequivocal benefits. The rediscovery of Turkic links from West China to the Balkans was the greatest novelty that the end of the Cold War brought to Turkey. Turkish and Western enthusiasm coincided in predicting a key role for Turkey in Central Asia. Ambitions in this area were understandable. With the exception of Tajikistan, all the new states were Turkic in language and culture and, where communism had not eroded it completely, Sunni Muslim in religion. Turks began to talk of "the Turkic world," and the 21st century being the "century of the Turk."[17] In March 1991 Ozal had pointedly visited Kiev and Almati during a visit to the Soviet Union. Even before their full independence, Turkey had discussed the possibility of providing military training, actively advocated the adoption of the Turkish (Latin) alphabet and script, and established plans for a satellite link to Central Asia that would carry Turkish broadcasts. By spring 1992 the leaders of all six former Soviet Muslim states had made official visits to Ankara. In May 1992 Demirel made a week-long visit to Central Asia, accompanied by a massive contingent of businessmen and political, economic, and cultural specialists. During this visit Demirel spoke of the possibility of establishing a Union of Turkish States. Thus, by the time of the first Turkic Summit in Ankara in November 1992, Turkey had made a bold bid for leadership and influence in the region, in the widest range of fields.

Regional Initiatives

The Black Sea Economic Co-operation Zone (BSECZ)
In 1990 Ozal initiated moves toward the regional integration of the countries surrounding the Black Sea. Initially talks included only Turkey, the Soviet Union, Bulgaria, and Romania, but the disintegration of the Soviet Union increased the number of participating states to nine, and the actual declaration was signed on 25 June 1992 by eleven countries (including Greece and Albania). The aim was to "create favourable conditions and establish institutional arrangements among the Black Sea countries for the development and diversification of their economic relations by making use of advantages arising from geographic proximity and the complementary nature of their economies."[18] Typical of an

Ozal initiative, it laid great stress on private enterprise in international co-operation. It encompassed an ambitious and extensive program, but explicitly stated that it was not in competition with existing integration programs (e.g., the EU), but was a complementary process to achieve a higher degree of integration into the Western economy. In line with the Ataturk 1930s Balkan Pact, the Turks also saw BSECZ as a vehicle for regional leadership, and another institution for promoting peace and stability in the region.

Water Pipelines for Peace

Water issues had always been a source of contention between Turkey, who owned the head-waters of the Euphrates and Tigris rivers, and Iraq and Syria, who relied on those waters for their irrigation. The ambitious and costly Southeast Anatolian Project (GAP) depended on the building of 22 dams in Southeast Turkey, including the giant Ataturk Dam. Although Turkey declared it would never use water as a political weapon, it had the powerful capability to cut off the flow of the Euphrates and had occasionally "controlled" the flow when filling reservoirs. Ozal could see the animosity this created, and in another of his creative departures, he suggested the construction of two water "peace pipelines" that would carry Anatolian water to Syria, Jordan and Israel, and to Saudi Arabia and the Gulf. In addition, he discussed with Syria the possibility of joint projects, including drinking water and electricity. This was unlikely to satisfy Syria, which continued to enlist Arab League support on water rights and which had never been reconciled to the loss of Hatay. In addition Syria had begun to use the increasingly violent Kurdish issue in Turkey as leverage on this issue.

Conclusion

Between 1990 and 1993 circumstances seemed to hold out a golden opportunity for Turkey to expand its influence and to carve out an important and unique regional role. Ozal had driven for it, public opinion had demanded it, and Turkey's friends had encouraged it. Despite a brief moment in the late 1980s, when a general enthusiasm for global trends had downgraded Turkey's strategic importance, it had been thrust to the center stage of a range of important issues. Ozal's vision had been to challenge the traditional maxim, "Turkey is a small power, which by definition (Rothstein's) implies that in general it is in the position of responding to what happens in the external environment rather than shaping that environment."[19] His aim had been to engage in a more active foreign policy in order to create a sphere of autonomous action that would both free Turkey from serving Western interests, yet at the same time increase its importance to the West. Ozal's actions in the Gulf crisis challenged the basic principles of Turkish foreign policy, and in both substance and style his conduct of foreign policy broke new ground. Across the region, in the Middle East, the Balkans, and the former Soviet Union he had launched initiatives and had set out a visionary and dynamic role for Turkey.

If this chapter has concentrated on Ozal it is because Ozal so dramatically drove the domestic and foreign policy agendas of Turkey at a time when the traditional political establishment was mesmerized by the dynamism of the new environment. In April 1993 Ozal embarked on an intensive tour of Central Asia. On 17 April, just after his return, he died. Diplomatic activity did not cease, engagement across a broad landscape of interests continued; yet, internally and externally it began to be recognized that the moment for Turkey to become a regional "power" seemed to have passed. Why?

Notes

1. The Azeris are Turkic but Shiites, the Chechens and Bosnians are Muslims but not Turkic, the Gagauz are Turkic but Christian.

2. Under this model foreign investors financed, built and operated a factory until they had recovered their investment and made an agreed profit. The business then was transferred to Turkish control.

3.   Duygu Sezer, *On the Faultlines of the Post Cold War Disorder,* in *Private View, The Quarterly International Review of TUSIAD* I, no. 1. (Winter 1996): 43.

4.   Interview with Cenghiz Candar, Foreign Affairs Editor, *Sabah* newspaper, 1 April 1996. Mr. Candar was one of President Ozal's foreign affairs advisers 1989-1993. Both he and Soli Ozel support the anecdote that in 1988 Ozal told the Manager of Turkish Airlines to look at Kazakhstan as a future base of Far East operations. Soli Ozel, "Of Not Being a Lone Wolf: Geography, Domestic Plays, and Turkish Foreign Policy in the Middle East," in *Powder Keg in the Middle East: The Struggle for Gulf Security,* eds, Geoffrey Kemp and Janice Gross Stein (London: Lanham, Rowman and Littlefield, 1995), 167.

5.   Between 1983 and 1993 trade between Turkey and the EU more than quadrupled to reach $20.2 billion. Sixty percent of foreign investment (1993, $4.6 billion) comes from member countries of the EU (Germany has the largest individual share), ahead of the United States (15 percent) and Japan (5 percent). Figures from the Assembly of Western European Union, *The Eastern Mediterranean, Document 1465,* 24 May 1995, 44.

6.   In 1978 Ecevit had rejected an offer to apply for full membership of the EEC, claiming that Turkey still needed a period of autarky for rapid industrialisation.

7.   In support of Turkey's application Ozal published a book in 1991 entitled, *Turkey in Europe, and Europe in Turkey* (Nicosia: K. Rustem and Brother, 1991).

8.   Kuniholm, "Turkey and the West," *Foreign Affairs* 70, no. 2 (1991): 36.

9.   Ozel, *Lone Wolf,* 170.

10.   Philip Robins, *Turkish Policy in the Gulf Crisis-Adventurist or Dynamic?* in *Turkish Foreign Policy: New Prospects,* ed. Clement H. Dodd (Wistow: Eothen Press, 1992), 72.

11.   Ibid., 70.

12.   While Ozal followed Ataturk's strictures against territorial ambition he had already told the United States in 1986 that if "Iran defeats Iraq and Iraq collapses, Turkey will claim back the Mosul region." Kuniholm, *Turkey and the West,* 44.

13.   Kemal Kirisci, *New Patterns of Turkish Foreign Policy Behaviour* in *Turkey: Economic, Political and Foreign Challenges for the 1990's,* ed. C. Karatus (Leiden: E. J. Brill, 1995), 4.

14.   *Turkish Daily News,* 14 April 1993.

15. Turkey estimates there are 2 million persons of Turkish origin in the Balkans (not all of them Muslim) and of the total Balkan population 9 million are Muslim. WEU, *The Eastern Mediterranean,* 38. There are also estimated to be 4 million Bosnian Muslims living in Turkey, who are affluent and vocal.

16. Suleiman Demirel, quoted in Hugh Pope, "Treading Softly in Armenia," in *Middle East International* 426 (29 May 1992).

17. Graham E. Fuller, "Turkey's New Eastern Orientation," in *Turkey's New Geopolitics,* 67.

18. Quoted in J. F. Brown, "Turkey: Back to the Balkans?," in *Turkey's New Geopolitics,* 156.

19. Duygu Sezer, "Turkey and the Western Alliance," in *The Political and Socio-Economic Transformation of Turkey,* eds. Atila Eralp, Muharrem Tunay, and Birol Yesilada (Westport, CT: Praeger, 1993), 216.

6.
Thwarted Ambition?

It was said of Margaret Thatcher, "She was more ambitious for the British people than they were for themselves." In a sense the same could have been said about Ozal. Despite the high-flown language of the popular press and the noisy acclamation of the masses for Turkey's new aspirations, those who actually wielded state power and who determined the speed at which ideas were translated into policy did not share his enthusiasm, and indeed viewed it as dangerous. No politician can act totally independently of his country's history, culture, and domestic politics. In Turkey this combination proved formidable in blunting many of Ozal's initiatives in both internal and foreign affairs. In addition, no country can for long act without regard for its geographical position and its resources. In assessing Turkey's post-Cold War security policy, the assertion, "The less you know about Turkey the more ambitious you are for her,"[1] has validity. It should not be viewed, however, as merely a negative statement. Ambitions do not need to be realistic to be sincerely held, but they do need to be realistic to be achievable. Despite the erosion of the Kemalist paradigm in many aspects, the state elite still retained their monopoly over security issues. Turkish ambition was therefore limited by the elite's continuing adherence to the self-imposed foreign policy constraints of Ataturk, but also by the hard facts of Turkey's geographical position, and its economic strength. External enthusiasts often overlooked the first, internal enthusiasts under-estimated the second.

Internal Politics

From as early as the October 1991 general elections, the conservative elements in the state coalesced to thwart Ozal's bolder initiatives. Despite Ozal's pre-eminent personal position, Demirel as the new prime minister, and Hikmet Cetin as the foreign minister, allied with the military to dominate the NSC. Having broken the old consensus during the Gulf War, Ozal did not have the time or the opportunity to reshape the internal structures of Turkey to provide a solid basis of support for his new vision. Demirel himself represented the archetypal Turkish politician: prepared to play to the crowd in the pursuit of political power, yet mainstream and conservative. He had an insular political vision and an understandable aversion to boldness. He had twice been ousted by the military and understood and accepted the limits that the political structure imposed on his actions. Ozal also understood the inseparable linkage between domestic and foreign policy, but sought to weaken that bond and reduce the limitations. He had deliberately concentrated on economic reform, and his extraordinary success had slowly enabled him to challenge the military's primacy in the state, allowing him to increase the areas of competence of the civil government. In 1987 he felt confident enough to recommend changes to the 1982 Constitution, and in 1991 had taken the unprecedented step of rejecting the army's nomination for Chief of TGS and appointing his own nominee. Gradually he took the lead in a growing number of decisions in the security and foreign affairs field, although this competence was never completed. However, Ozal failed to convince the elite that Turkey's aspiration to "regional power" status required a radical reordering of domestic politics. Nor, despite popular acclaim, was he able to appeal over their heads to the electorate for this mandate.

This is not to say that without Ozal Turkish foreign policy would have been quiescent. The new environment made a static position impossible, and public opinion demanded activity; therefore, the DYP government was very active in foreign affairs. Demirel who had a reputation for hardly ever travelling in the 1960s and 1970s, attended numerous international meetings and paid official visits to many countries. This program did not slacken after he was elected president, and his foreign minister made 44 official overseas visits in 1992 alone. This activity across the range of Turkey's international interests continued through the Ciller government era. It was given further impetus by Turkey's move to join the European Customs Union in 1995, thereby completing the 22-year process begun with the 1963 Ankara Agreement. However, the mainstream elements of Turkish political life did not share Ozal's grandiose vision of a dynamic, multifaceted regional role. Their aim remained to keep a Western orientation as the "permanent" policy of the Republic, while as a new "temporary" policy they would seek to "manage" the changed international environment in a manner that did not endanger Turkish security, nor left them without allies. Their aspirations were therefore more realistic and consistent with the traditional bases of Turkish goals, if less exciting than Ozal's. Set against the earlier rhetoric, from 1993 onwards Turkey's wide-ranging foreign policy activity seemed to generate fewer and fewer results, leading to the accusation, or merely assessment, that Turkish foreign policy had somehow "failed."[2] This was unfair. Between 1989 and 1996 there were eight different governments and twelve MFAs. It is a tribute to the professionalism of the MFA civil service that Turkish foreign policy did not oscillate wildly through this period and that Turkey survived this completely new phase of its history without incurring great risks, or making great mistakes.

The Economy

The parlous state of the economy had been a prime cause of the political polarization of politics in the 1970s, and the subsequent intervention by the military. Statism had been tempered under the Menderes regime of the 1950s but it was not seriously challenged until Ozal. Turkey's elite had always been military men and civil servants, and their grasp of economics was weak, but Ozal understood Ataturk's circular argument regarding security, development, strength, and security. He also knew that Turkey's poor economic record was the product of outdated political constraints on economic development. Ozal sought to abandon 60 years of statist policies and move decisively to a free-market economy. In Turkish terms he was strikingly successful. By 1991 the average growth through the decade had been nearly 8 percent, per capita gross national product (GNP) had doubled from $1,300 to $2,600, and purchasing power parity had also doubled. The agriculture share of GNP fell from 22 to 16 percent. In 1980 exports totalled $2.9 billion, with agricultural produce constituting 57 percent. In 1991 exports were worth $13.6 billion, with the agricultural share falling to 19.7 percent. In the same period imports rose from $7.9 to $21 billion, and energy accounted for nearly 20 percent of this total. Tourism, remittances from workers abroad, and Turkish contracting work, particularly in construction, all contributed to the growing Turkish economy. Within Turkey extensive infrastructure works were begun, including the enormous GAP project.

In absolute terms the figures were impressive, but in relative terms they were not good enough to give Turkey the room for the maneuver it needed in its two most important areas of foreign policy concern: as a regional power and as a candidate for EU membership. Turkey's economic success was hampered by persistent high inflation, slowness in privatization, widening budget deficits, and mounting external debt. In December 1989 the European Commission declined to open negotiations on Ozal's 1987 application for full EU membership. They cited Turkey's low- level economic development (half the per capita GDP of the EU's poorest countries), high population growth (2.5 percent per annum, 10 times the EU average!), the long-term foreign debt ($38 billion, the world's seventh largest), low tax revenue and high state expenditure (over twice the EU average), a state sector continuing to account for 40 percent of manufacturing output (despite Ozal's privatization), and soaring, unpredictable inflation. Even the positive sides of Turkey's situation acted against it. Turkey was one of the world's most favored agricultural nations and its membership would increase the EU's usable agricultural area by 22 percent, thereby doubling European output of a variety of important products, of no benefit to anyone. Not the least problem was the prospect of granting free movement of Turkish labor at a time when immigration had emerged as a controversial issue across Europe.[3]

In addition, despite the clear economic advantages of privatization and reduction of the state sector, Ozal's free market economic philosophy was challenged at home. It flew in the face of those with an ideological or financial stake in statism. In a country where a job with "the government," however lowly or poorly paid, gave status and security, there was suspicion of the harsh realities of the private sector. Reforms also created a very obviously wealthy class, whose ostentation inflamed a traditional Turkish low regard for businessmen. Combined with mass migration of poor, conservative peasants from the country to the cities, these prejudices created further social tension. A thriving and dynamic private sector did grow, but despite Ozal's reforms, the state was not in a position to profit from this dynamism. Partly this resulted from tax evasion and inefficient revenue collection, and partly it was the continued squandering of revenue on the remaining large, unproductive state sector. Even under Ozal the financial and fiscal discipline vital for success of the economic reform program was weakened by the pressures of domestic politics.

The situation was exacerbated by the Gulf War and the three-way embargo on Iraq, Armenia, and Serbia. Ozal had gambled that a firm, early commitment to the U.S. coalition would be properly rewarded; it was not. The closure of the oil pipeline, along with the loss of Middle East trade was estimated to have cost Turkey $9 billion in lost revenue by the end of 1991. By the end of 1995 estimated losses were $30 billion. Contributions from the Gulf states, re-building contracts, and arms transfers all helped, but many of the Turks who condemned Ozal's precipitous support of the United States justifiably believed they would never be adequately compensated for the economic and long-term security consequences of their cooperative role.

The death of Ozal in April 1993 removed much of the remaining impetus behind government reform of the Turkish public sector. Demirel, and his DYP successor Tansu Ciller, never had the same ideological commitment to privatization, or were prepared to impose the necessary discipline on the economy. In 1995 Ciller compounded the problems when she responded to public sector disturbances by raising wages and reducing retirement ages. By the general election of December 1995 Turkey was living beyond its means, and the distortions in its economy continued to be structural and endemic. The government and state economic enterprises were all operating under deficits that could no longer be financed by taxes. The Central Bank was printing money, which was fueling an inflation rate of over 100 percent, and the government was being forced to borrow money at increasing rates of interest. This in turn siphoned off resources from the private, productive sector. The obvious economic solutions of further, fast privatization and a complete overhaul of the social security system both carried political and social costs that the weak DYP government and the shaky DYP-ANAP coalition of 1996 were simply not prepared to address,[4] nor were the Kemalist Democratic Socialist Party (DSP), on whose support the coalition depended. Almost the first action of the Refah-DYP government was to raise civil service salaries by 50 percent, with little indication how this would be financed. Therefore economic weakness continued to have its effect on Turkey's foreign policy aspirations. Not only did it undermine acceptance in Western economic institutions, but Turkey increasingly found that it thwarted attempts to exert regional influence. The appeal of ethnic and religious solidarity in Central Asia simply could not compete with the financial clout of the United States, Japan, South Korea, and Western Europe. Nor could Turkey fill the ambitious leadership role in the BSECZ that it had charted for itself.

Refah Alters the Equation

Economic change and weakness also influenced domestic politics. From the initiation of multiparty politics in 1946 there had always been Islamists in the political system, either represented in the wing of a mainstream party or, when not officially banned by the military, as a party in their own right. In 1987 Ozal had amended the 1982 Constitution to lift the ban on certain political individuals (Demirel and Erbakan among them) and permit a revived Islamist party to form, the Refah Party. Islamists had always opposed the state's adherence to a Western orientation but, except in coalition through the fractious period of the 1970s, and on the issue of Cyprus, their influence on foreign policy had been minimal. From 1992 onward their voice was increasingly heard, either expounding their own vision of Turkey's foreign policy orientation or berating the government's perceived foreign policy failures. Refah supporters could discern the economic advantages of links to the West, and some respected the political institutions of the West, but they were more influenced by historical, cultural, philosophical and religious differences.

In addition to its religious followers, Refah gathered votes from those who saw themselves as disenfranchised by traditional politics, concerned at the consequences of economic reform, or scornful of corruption and ostentatious wealth. Sponsored and subsidized by other Islamic countries, they used the natural organizational advantages of religion and took these into the political arena. In many ways their position was analogous to that of the Euro-Communists in Italy in the 1970s. They sought to provide good, competent, uncorrupt local government which contrasted with the "pork barrel" politics of the mainstream secular parties. In March 1994,

Refah won 17.98 percent of the popular vote in the local elections. This success gave Refah 327 mayorships covering 40 million people, including control of the municipalities of Ankara and Istanbul.[5] There had been a gradual re-Islamisation of Turkey since the early 1980s, but this had been broadly controlled by the state. By 1994, the secular establishment at last were forced to accept that the country's politics had changed.

In 1994 the Refah appeal was based on domestic issues and advocating "Just Order." But they also had a well developed foreign policy that reflected their Islamic consciousness and fed on Turkish sympathies for Muslim "victims" in Bosnia and Chechenya. Refah claimed to believe that the international system was run by the United States and Israel to the detriment of the *Ummah*. This axis aimed to maintain global domination by thwarting the ability of the *Ummah* to exercise their potential, which was now even greater with the collapse of communism. Therefore, the U.S. approach to Islam was to suppress those countries where it was an active, independent force (Libya, Iran, Sudan), and to restrict Islamic influence in those countries where the governing forces were compliant with U.S. interests (Turkey, Egypt, Jordan). Refah believed that the importation of Western institutions and mores ran counter to Islamic tradition and that the Kemalist elite were not secular in a Western sense, but actively antireligious and therefore perverted Turkish society by not allowing free expression of Islamic thought in Muslim Turkey. The solution was to redress the balance in Turkey by developing an Islamic orientation in society. At the same time, greater social, political, and economic cooperation should take place among the *Ummah*, and this co-ordination would require the creation of international Islamic institutions to parallel those in the West.[6]

While Erbakan moderated his demands when faced with the prospect of sharing coalition power after Refah success in the December 1995 elections, he was on record as advocating an Islamic United Nations, EU, and NATO. In addition, Refah proposed to scrap the majority of defense contracts with the West, terminate Operation *Provide Comfort*, reopen trade with Iraq, and renegotiate the 1995 Customs Union. The general thrust behind these proposals was encompassed in his statement "when we come to power we will no longer be the servant, the slave of the West."[7] Elements of this package had a surprisingly broad appeal in Turkish society since their program appealed to the deep-rooted, historical Turkish suspicion of foreigners, experience of economic humiliation, and resistance to a subordinate position vis-a-vis the West. Despite this, the Refah leadership claimed to accept that Turkey was part of Europe and that they had no intention of isolating Turkey from the West, although they saw no chance of Turkey joining the EU. Nor did they intend to take Turkey out of NATO, which they recognized as important for Turkish security and a bulwark against Communists, Leftists, and Marxists.[8]

Refah declared themselves to be the only party in Turkey that genuinely supported a civil society that was dominant over the state ideology. They wanted to amend the Constitution to curtail the influence of the military in the NSC and to subordinate the Chief of TGS to the MOD, "as in other Western democratic countries." Refah totally opposed the Marxist-Leninist Kurdish Workers Party (PKK), but they recognized a separate Kurdish identity that must be incorporated within Turkey. Although they criticized the way the military conducted operations in the Southeast, they, too, had concern over threats to the unity and integrity of the country. Along with the Cyprus problem, only the Kurdish issue, and the related problem of PKK terrorism, could produce an unlikely community of interest between the Army and an Islamic party.

The Armed Forces

The military's place and role in Turkish society had been enshrined by Ataturk and reinforced by their interventions into domestic politics. For the majority of Turks, the military had successfully defended Turkey against external threat, re-

77

established stability during periods when the democratic process had failed, and decisively intervened to save the Turkish Cypriots. Their place on the NSC guaranteed their veto on security issues, and from 1974 they controlled the National Security assessment. In 1981 they embarked fully on the REMO program, assisted by the "second Cold War," and the resumption of U.S. aid. In the period 1985-1990 modernization costs were nearly $15 billion, of which about $5 billion came from the United States and Germany. This is not a large sum by Western standards, but by 1986 the defense budget was estimated to be taking more than 25 percent of the national budget, when U.S. and German aid was included.[9]

The end of the Cold War came as a mixed blessing for the military. With their MFA colleagues they were concerned at Turkey's downgraded strategic position and wary of Ozal's plans for an expanded regional role. For nearly 70 years the Army had adopted a defensive posture.[10] They appreciated that a direct military and ideological threat to the "West," of which it was a part, had been lifted, but this now placed Turkey firmly in one of the least stable areas of the world. In line with the 1989 foreign policy assessment, the military had negotiated an opt-out in the Conventional Forces in Europe (CFE) Agreement that excluded its troops in the Southeast on the borders of Iraq and Syria. Its threat perception and the war against the PKK denied Turkey the opportunity to benefit from any "peace dividend." Indeed TGS saw the performance of the coalition forces in the Gulf War as demanding a further major restructuring and modernization program. Contingency planning in 1990 for a move on the Kirkut oil fields had revealed how inflexible their organization was, and how deficient they were in equipment for operational mobility and logistic support.

In the 1995 Turkish Defense Statement, the preamble rehearsed the facts of the new security environment but concluded by stating: "Under these circumstances, it would not be an overstatement to claim that the major factors affecting Turkey's defence policy and doctrine have remained

78

the same over decades. The main reason for this is the geopolitical location of the country and the dynamics and the history of the region."[11] On this basis the defense policy supported the multilateral approach of foreign policy and continued to be based on Ataturk's dictum "Peace at Home, Peace in the World." The principles were:

- To preserve and secure the independence, integrity and the democratic (and secular) regime of the Republic of Turkey
- To take all precautionary measures to prevent crises and war
- To participate actively in collective defense and peace-keeping activities
- To contribute to decreasing international tension and to ensure just and permanent peace.

To carry out these policy objectives the Turkish Armed Forces had developed four pillars of defense strategy:

- Deterrence: in the form of participation in collective defense (primarily NATO)
- Restructuring: re-equipment and organizational change to ensure mobility and flexibility of response to the multiple threats that exist to the country (internal and external).
- Crisis Response: The Turkish Armed Forces would be ready and prepared to respond, both regionally and globally, to any threat to peace.
- Forward Defense: Turkey perceived no buffer zone and saw increased risks and threats since the end of the Cold War, and therefore retained a policy of forward defense.

In broad terms, in 1996 the Turkish Armed Forces were the predominant military force in the Balkans, Trans-Caucasus, and the Middle East. They could field over a million men, approximately 3,400 tanks, and more than 360 modern, front-line aircraft.[12] The "upside" of the CFE agreement was that between 1991 and 1993 TGS were able to take full advantage of the NATO "cascade" program, receiving nearly $8 billion worth of U.S. and German equipment, including nearly 1,000

M-60s and 100 Leopard tanks. In addition the ongoing modernization program aimed to procure 1,700 armored infantry fighting vehicles, multilaunch rocket systems, and attack and support helicopters, while continuing to produce the F-16 fighter.

Despite these capabilities, the military had little stake in an ambitious foreign policy which might threaten national security or isolate it in the region. The requirement for alliances was vital, given Turkey's security concerns on its borders. However, within this well-defined defensive role, there was increasing talk of the requirement to be able to conduct a 2½ war strategy.[13] In line with the 1989 MFA assessment this was predicated on Syria and Greece supporting each other to take advantage of Turkey's problems in the Southeast. The military would therefore have to fight on two fronts while containing an insurgency. The military training agreement between Greece and Syria in March 1995 seemed to support these fears. Turkey's response was to intensify military contacts with Israel, a move clearly aimed at Syria and provoking criticism throughout the Arab world.

The Defense Budget

Broadly speaking, TGS always received the budget allocation they requested, but the total allocation for defense remained a secret, figures were difficult to interpret, and there was no full transparency of defense spending. In the 1990s, according to official figures, defense normally accounted for 12 percent of the national budget, 2 percent of GNP, and 4.5 percent of GDP.[14] Inflation, and the costs of the war in the Southeast, further distorted a proper assessment of the figures, but some estimates suggest that by 1996 total "security" costs were as high as 35 percent of all government spending. The armed forces were financed from three main sources: the defense budget; foreign aid, including "cascade" equipment and remaining Gulf War reimbursements; and the Defense Industries Support Fund for the Under Secretary for Defense

Industries (SSM). The latter, designed to help develop an economically viable, indigenous defense manufacturing industry, received a special development fund outside the allocation in the state budget for procurement of equipment.[15] Of the budget, 40 to 45 percent was for staff expenses, 50 to 54 percent for training, equipment and running costs, and the rest for investment and transfer expenses.

By 1995, along with the PKK problem in the Southeast, the military's overriding concern was the economy. Rampant inflation drastically reduced the purchasing power of those on state incomes and began to cause great dissatisfaction among the professional officer and NCO corps.[16] Ciller's 1995 austerity package meant that, for the first time, the Treasury scrutinized aspects of the defense budget and trimmed procurement funds from $3.25 to $2.25 billion. Defense projects had to be cancelled or deferred, while the rising costs of combating the PKK took a larger and larger proportion of the budget, delaying the modernization and re-structuring program. In the broader picture the military could see that inflation, economic failure, and political corruption was contributing to the rise in support for the Refah Party, who openly challenged the Western-oriented, secular basis of Turkish society, and therefore challenged the military.

Refah and the Military

In December 1995 Refah took 21.38 percent of the popular vote in the general election, making them the single largest party in the GNA, with 158 seats.[17] In the same month the Army pointedly and publicly dismissed 50 officers and sergeants for overzealous religious observance. At the same time, as had been seen after Refah's local government success, many officers began to wear Ataturk lapel badges. The official reaction to the military's reaction to the election result was "we are watching." President Demirel asked Erbakan and Refah, as the largest party, to form a government. His failure came as little surprise to "Turkey-watchers," but February, when the prospect of an ANAP-Refah coalition was possible, the Chief of TGS, General Karadayi, and his commanders visited the Speaker of the GNA. The latter sought to assure them that he would pay particular attention to the protection of Kemalist secularism and the Western-oriented principles of government.[18] Before this visit the military had commissioned and published an opinion poll that concluded that the majority (59.5 percent) wanted an ANAP-DYP coalition.[19] The assumption was that the military had no ambition to intervene in politics again, but did not want to be put in a position where they might have to do so. The intended message was clear. The Islamists must be kept out of power until the secular mainstream could pull itself together. Therefore the discreet hand of the military was seen in the deal whereby Ciller and Yilmaz put aside personal animosity to form a coalition. Even then Army-Islamist tension did not go away, and in March 1996, when the Gendarmerie issued a circular banning soldiers from using the mosques in the barracks, Refah spokesmen accused the military of being anti-religious. This provoked a quick and harsh response from TGS, and Erbakan, anxious for power and fully aware of the military's sentiments, was equally quick to distance himself from the remarks and to forbid his party to make further statements concerning the Army.[20]

The collapse of the ANAP-DYP coalition in June 1996 was a grave disappointment to the military, and to all those who had voted for secular parties. Given the personal animosities of all the secular party leaders, it began to appear that any government would have to include Refah in coalition. Opinion was divided on the Army's reaction. Turkish national papers claimed that:

- The military's stance on Refah was softening, with a senior officer saying "It is time they came to power, if they do not come to power now . . . they will do so at the next election, and with an explosive increase in votes."
- A Refah government would lead to a military coup.
- Another military source had said "the Army's attitude will depend on the way Refah act."[21]

As it became clearer that Refah would lead a government, the military publicly renounced any intention of intervention but privately made clear to Erbakan the constraints and limitations on his actions if he led a new government. By the time the Refah-DYP coalition won a vote of confidence on 8 July 1996, Erbakan had agreed that DYP would hold the Foreign, Defense and Interior portfolios and had changed his position on most security issues. Turkey would remain in NATO and the Customs Union, Operation *Provide Comfort* would be extended (under new arrangements), the details of the Turco-Israeli military agreement would be "considered," and the military's attitude to the Kurdish issue would be respected.

The Kurdish Issue

The founding principles of the Turkish Republic barred the political expression of four ideologies: Islamism, communism, liberalism, and Kurdish nationalism. By 1990 three of these bans were largely meaningless, but that on Kurdish nationalism remained. Discriminated against as an ethnic group from the foundation of the Republic, Kurdish tribal organization and cultural identity never sat well with the centralised, nation-state secularism of the new Republic. In the 1970s and 1980s there was a worrying resurgence of traditional Kurdish unrest in Southeast Anatolia. The collapse of the Turkish economy in the 1970s had been particularly harshly felt in the Kurdish areas, and in the general anarchy that prevailed, Kurdish separatist violence also grew. This was seen by the military not simply as a challenge to state authority, but also a direct and real threat to the integrity of the unitary Turkish state, whose defense they were constitutionally charged with. Between 1980 and 1983, the military government was particularly heavy handed in the suppression of the Kurds in the Southeast.

The PKK were officially founded in 1978, but in 1984 Abdullah Ocalan re-launched a guerrilla campaign committed to achieving a separate Kurdish state and was supported in their actions against the Turkish state by Syria, Iraq, Iran and the Soviet Union.[22] Funding came from a variety of sources, most notably from Kurds in Germany.[23] In bald figures, by 1996 the PKK had between 4,000-10,000 men under arms, perhaps half of them at any one time in Turkey. Through genuine commitment, or fear, their supporters numbered up to 400,000. At least 200,000 troops were involved in security operations, with an additional 45,000 village guards, at an annual cost to the state of $4 to $7 billion. Up to 3,000 villages had been destroyed or evacuated, perhaps 20,000 people killed, and up to a million people emigrated to the cities, further exacerbating urban social problems. The Kurdish issue, initially viewed by the army as a straightforward domestic security matter, became the focus of all Turkey's internal and external concerns. It challenged the roots of Turkish identity and security, the role of the state in society, the nature of its democracy, the economic health and development of Turkey, its relations with the West from a human rights angle, and the rest of the region from a security perspective.

This terrorism, and the state's response to it, has had extremely damaging consequences for the fabric of Turkish society. The war has been fought with utmost brutality, and the calculated atrocities of the PKK have provoked a similarly violent response from the security forces. Any element of "hearts and minds" in the military campaign has been difficult to discern. The barbarism of the PKK has been beyond doubt, but there has been widespread evidence of security force involvement in killings and torturing, and by 1995 few members of the security forces had been punished for human rights abuses.[24] The equal culpability of both sides was not seen in the West, where a broad coalition of anti-Turkish lobbies has used the Kurdish issue to castigate Turkey, thereby undermining other foreign policy ambitions.

The costs of the war have distorted both the national and the defense budgets, but there were other significant costs. The war fueled enmity between Turks and Turks of Kurdish origin, in other parts of Turkey, who had lived side by side for decades. Tourism revenues fell, and the broader problems of political relations with the West seemed overlarge, particularly in Germany where the Turk-Kurd violence found its way onto the streets. Although Britain, France, Germany and the United States banned the PKK as a terror group, a significant proportion of Turkish public opinion saw the presence of Kurdish support groups in the West as confirmation of their old suspicion that the "West" was sympathetic to a separate Kurdish state.[25] External attitudes to the Kurdish issue began to replace Cyprus as the touchstone of whether a country was "friendly" to Turkey or not. This Sevres-phobic approach, with its obsession with territorial integrity, accounted for the strange coalition of Kemalists, nationalists, Islamists, Social Democrats, and the Army over this issue.

Despite the determination to treat the Kurdish issue as a military problem, TGS and the NSC must have discerned that Turkish security and diplomatic power was being severely undermined by the disproportionate allocation of resources to the struggle in the Southeast. From 1993 the military operations in the region were prosecuted much more effectively, and the Army gained enormous experience in counterinsurgency operations. Ponderous by modern standards, Operation *Steel*, launched against the PKK bases in Northern Iraq in March-April 1995, was businesslike, well coordinated, and effective. However, the failure to launch any parallel program of social, economic or cultural initiatives showed a continuing disregard of the underlying nonmilitary dimensions of the problem. The Turkish state, with wide public support, continued with the assumption that "the Kurdish problem for Turkey was in essence that of an estranged minority operating beyond the frontier, under the patronage of Turkey's hostile Middle Eastern neighbors."[26]

Between 1990 and 1993 there was a chance of an accommodation with the Kurds, if not the PKK. Ozal's political predominance gave him the authority to challenge the accepted norms. The fiction of "Mountain Turks" was discarded, and the problem was increasingly referred to as "the Kurdish issue" in the media. In 1990 Ozal rescinded the constitutional ban on "non-Turkish languages." In October 1991 Demirel took up the theme stating that "Turkey has recognized the reality of its Kurdish population." The scope for maneuvre however, was limited by the attitudes of the military, and extremists on both sides. The Kurdish Nevruz celebrations of March 1992 were the scene of violent clashes that left 92 dead and 341 wounded. The military demanded the right to a free hand again and the DYP government gave it to them. Nineteen ninety-two was the bloodiest year of the insurgency, with up to 4,000 deaths and a major intervention by the Turkish army into Iraq.[27] In this they were supported by the local Kurdish Democratic Party (KDP), who were supplied and protected by TGS under the auspices of Operation *Provide Comfort*.[28] Thus, the Kurdish issue and the aftermath of the Gulf War became inextricably entangled.[29] The opportunity to take advantage of Ocalan's unilateral cease-fire in March 1993 was lost when Ozal died in April of the same year.

Ozal inspires speculative theories. Some have suggested that he accepted the inevitability of some degree of autonomy for the Kurds. Combined with a collapse of central authority in Iraq, he could contemplate a Kurdish state carved out of the four countries their ethnic homeland covered. Such a scenario held less terror for him than for the Kemalists, for he saw Turkey being the dominant influence over any new Kurdish state, perhaps even to the extent of gaining control over the still coveted Mosul region.[30] If his vision was not that dramatic, Ozal was still confident no Kurdish state could be formed against Turkey's will.[31] Whether he could ever have gained acceptance of a radical solution on these lines is problematic. On his death, Turkish politics returned to their more conventional pattern, and Tansu Ciller established a close relationship with General Dogan Gures, the new Chief of TGS. While such matters can only be taken on assumption in Turkish politics, there was no doubt that a free hand in the Southeast was the price of full military support of the DYP administration. Gures' infusion of new tactics, more soldiers, improved command and control, and better equipment undoubtedly contributed to the greater military success, but as commented on above, there appeared to be no civil initiatives to capitalize on the military stability achieved in the area. At the same time Turkey began to purchase Russian equipment, which, unlike U.S. and German weapon systems, did not come with any restrictions on their use.[32]

Notes

1. Quoted by Anthony Cordesman, Senior Analyst, CSIS, Washington, 21 February 1996.

2. The Russian Naval Attaché said that "by watching the Turkish foreign policy I have at last understood the Olympic principle; it's not the winning that counts, but the taking part in as many sports as possible." Captain Mikail Popov, Ankara, 8 December 1995.

3. Ian O. Lesser, "Bridge or Barrier? Turkey and the West after the Cold War," in *Turkey's New Geopolitics*, 104-107.

4. Interview with George Zaidan, Southeast Europe Regional Director, World Bank, 22 February 1996.

5. Philip Robins, *Political Islam: The Rise of the Welfare Party*, January 1995, 2.

6. Interview with Ali Sarikaya, Refah Party HQ, Istanbul, 5 July 1996.

7. *Turkish Daily News*, 6 January 1996.

8. Interview with Dr Abdullah Gul, Deputy Chairman, Refah, Istanbul, 8 April 1996.

9. Mehmet Ali Birand, *Shirts of Steel, An Anatomy of the Turkish Armed Forces* (London and New York: I.B. Tauris, 1991), 202.

10. Although successful, the 1974 intervention in Cyprus revealed many weaknesses in the Turkish military's grasp of modern, joint, offensive operations.

11. Taken from a draft copy of the 1995 Turkish Defense Statement, *Part One, New Security Environment*, 3.

12. Figures taken from 1995 IISS Strategic Balance.

13. Sukru Elekdag, "2 1/2 War Strategy," in *Perceptions, Journal of International Affairs* 1, no. 1 (March-May 1996): 33-57. This article reflects a growing conviction that, in the final analysis, most of the threats facing Turkey will have to be met by Turkey on its own.

14. 1995 (draft) Defense Statement, 83-86.

15. This money comes from a proportion of the taxes paid on fuel, tobacco, alcohol, the lottery and the tote. At its best it contributed $700 million per year, but inflation had eroded this to $500 million in 1994. Another institution that distinguishes the Turkish armed forces from other armies is the Army Aid Fund (Turkish initials: OYAK). Founded in 1961 it is funded from monthly payments by Turkish officers and NCOs and is authorized to engage in all types of industrial and commercial activity. It owns buildings, real estate and companies. Unofficially its assets are believed to be measured in billions of dollars. Proceeds fund a range of military welfare projects.

16. Between January and June 1994, real wages in Turkey fell by over 30 percent, particularly hitting the purchasing power of those in the public sector. Asaf Akat, "Turkey at the Crossroads," in *Private View, The Quarterly Review of TUSIAD* I, no. 1 (Winter 1996) 24-26.

17. Ciller's DYP took 19.18 percent of the vote with 135 seats, Yilmaz's ANAP 19.65 percent but only 132 seats, and Ecevit's DSP gained 14.64 percent of the vote and 76 seats.

18. Turkish Probe, 9 February 1996, 5.

19. Ibid., 6.

20. *Hurriyet*, 28 March 1996, and *Probe*, no. 172 (29 March 1996): 17.

21. Milliyet, SABAH, and Cumhuriyet, quoted in *Turkish Daily News*, 10 June 1996.

22. Syria provides bases for the PKK in the Bekaa Valley and, despite denials, Ocalan has a flat in Damascus. Syria, Iraq and Iran have all exploited the PKK at various stages to put pressure on the Turkish government, often over the issue of water rights. The Armenian terror group ASALA certainly had links with the PKK. In recent months Turkey has also accused Greece of harboring the PKK.

23. There are 400,000 Turks of Kurdish origin in Germany, 60,000 in France, and 10,000 in Sweden. They form an important anti-Turkish lobby in Western Europe.

24. MFA figures claim 1194 cases and 15 convictions in 1994, and 962 cases and 20 convictions in 1995. "Turkey Survey," in *The Economist*, 8 June 1996, 14.

25. The issue of MED-TV, a satellite broadcasting company, based in the United Kingdom and dedicated to Kurdish "cultural" affairs, has caused major difficulties between Britain and Turkey. One Turk said "Just wait until we are transmitting "IRA-TV" to you, and see how you like it!"

26. Philip Robins, "The Overlord State: Turkish Policy and the Kurdish Issue," *International Affairs* 69.4 (1993), 669.

27. Ibid., 667.

28. Operation *Provide Comfort* is often referred to in the Turkish press as "Poised Hammer."

29. The situation on the Turkish-Iraqi border is very complicated. Since the Saadabad Pact of 1937 the Turks and Iraqis had an agreement that let them both deal with their Kurdish minorities. In 1985 they agreed a "hot pursuit" policy that suited Saddam Hussein who was then at war with Iran. In 1988 Saddam's crushing of a Kurdish uprising led to a massive influx of Kurds into Southeast Turkey. It was to prevent a repetition of this that underlay Turkish support for the "Safe Havens" proposal, which led to Operation *Provide Comfort.* In the nature of Kurdish tribal politics, this Northern Iraqi area was divided between the competing factions of the Kurdish Democratic Party (KDP), led by Masoud Barzani, and the Patriotic Union of Kurdistan (PUK) under Jalal Talebani.

30. Interview with Cenghiz Candar 1 April 1996.

31. Soli Ozel, "Of Not Being a Lone Wolf: Geography, Domestic Plays, and Turkish Foreign Policy in the Middle East," in *Powder Keg in the Middle East: The Struggle for Gulf Security,* eds, Geoffrey Kemp and Janice Gross Stein (London: Lanham, Rowman and Littlefield, 1995), 180.

32. Interview with General Dogan Gures, Ankara, 8 April 1996. Gures stood as a DYP deputy in the December 1995 elections. There was speculation that, if Ciller had led the ANAP-DYP coalition, it would have brought Gures in as the MOD. This may have been done with the aim of beginning a process under which the military answer to a civilian chief. In the vote of confidence for the Refah-DYP coalition Gures absented himself. While many presidents have been military men, there seems to be a general dislike among army officers that General Gures had gone into electoral politics.

7.
Bridge or Barrier?[1]

In March 1996 the ANAP-DYP coalition government under Mesut Yilmaz set out its foreign policy priorities. The program represented a broad, center-right foreign policy agenda. The preamble declared that Turkey was an inalienable part of Europe, but also a Middle Eastern and Asian state. As such it provided an area of stability between the Balkans and the Caucasus. The list of objectives, which must be assumed to be in some order of priority, read:

- Resolution of the EU membership issue
- Greater weight to economic relations with the United States
- Increased cooperation with Russia
- Greater engagement in Central Asia and Azerbaijan, including measures to resolve the situations regarding Nagorno-Karabakh and Chechenya
- Relations with Islamic and Middle East states
- A warning to all states supporting terrorism in Turkey
- The question of Iraq and the status of Operation *Provide Comfort*
- Bosnia
- A declared intention to be active in international organizations.

In a special section, the program listed Greece, Cyprus, and Human Rights, pointedly stating that human rights issues were being pursued for their own sake, not because of the pressures of Western governments.[2] There was no mention of the Kurdish issue in any section of the government program.

The last formal statement of foreign policy objectives had been in 1991, under Demirel's DYP government. While it was a conventional official document, it reflected greater confidence having successfully gambled on an active policy in the Gulf War, and in anticipation of the dissolution of the Soviet Union. It was less ambitious than Ozal might have been, but it was issued as a realistic, achievable program, based on the assumption that Turkey would and could shape its foreign policy environment. This confidence lasted until about 1993. The 1996 program lacked this confidence, exuding a more traditional, passive, and defensive note. It was minimalist and less pro-active. Not only did it reflect the internal, structural limitations on an active Turkish foreign policy, but it also acknowledged the realities of Turkey's geopolitical position which militated against its achievement of a dynamic, forward-leaning policy.

Turkey's Relations With the West

Turkey and the United States

The Republican administrations of both Reagan and Bush had been sympathetic to Turkey, particularly in the wake of the Iranian revolution. The United States recognized Turkey's role as a regional stabilizer long before the collapse of the Soviet Union. Despite the ups and downs of this relationship, Turkey's support was important in an area where U.S. commitments were complicated by the clash between its dependency on Arab oil and its policy of supporting Israel. The active role of Turkey in the Gulf War had enhanced this position. Both Ozal and Bush had agreed that Turkey could act as the new role model for the Trans-Caucasus and Central Asia. Not only would this assist both countries, but it might limit a revival of Russian influence in these areas and counter the radical Islamic influence of Iran. In the Middle East, Turkey would develop its relations with Egypt and Israel in support of the Peace Process, and in addition to hosting Operation *Provide Comfort*, they would assist the U.S. policy of dual-containment of Iran and Iraq. The quid-pro-quo would be U.S.

support of Turkey's regional ambitions, and full compensation for its Gulf War support.

Despite regular congressional criticism of Turkey, Republican administrations had normally bypassed Democrat obstructions. If Bush had won the 1992 election, the ambitions of both Ozal and the Republicans may have come closer to fruition, but instead, Clinton won the presidency. Democratic control of both the executive and legislature was unfortunate for Turkey. Not only was Clinton's administration committed to concentrating on domestic issues, particularly the economy, but it was significantly influenced by anti-Turkish lobby groups.[3] Turkey had by this stage adopted a forward regional position and felt exposed, as the military and MFA had feared it would be. Turkish public opinion felt betrayed. Inflated rhetoric and promises had been based on an assumption of U.S. financial and political support. They now appeared to be left with only the downsides of their multidirectional policy.[4] The United States remained the most important Turkish bilateral relationship, but new irritations compounded traditional ambivalence. Those who wanted to sustain this vitally important axis were hampered by the domestic politics of both countries. The United States was prepared to keep underwriting the Turkish military, but Congress demanded that no military assistance should go to Turkey without strings attached regarding human rights and limitations on where equipment could be used. The Turkish Government and military still wanted this aid, but publicizing this assistance and the accompanying caveats drew criticism that the government was once again compromising Turkey's sovereignty, and placing it in a position of subservience to the United States. U.S. policy and public opinion demanded the dual-containment of Iran and Iraq and the maintenance of Operation *Provide Comfort*. The benefits for Turkey were less obvious. Cost, compromised sovereignty, distorted relations with Arab neighbors, and the Sevres-phobia of an assault on Turkey's territorial integrity were all accusations thrown at the government as these policies continued.

93

Across a range of other issues, the limitations of US support were seen. From 1992 the West saw the priority foreign policy objective as the consolidation of democracy in Russia. In the interests of this, the West was prepared to make a range of compromises and concessions that Turkey saw as impinging on areas of its legitimate concern. They included relaxing the CFE restrictions on the "flanks," being oversensitive to Russian support for the Serbs in the Balkan conflict, turning a blind eye to Russian activities in the "near abroad," and a muted response to the brutal suppression of the Chechen revolt. In each of these issues Turkey felt increasingly it was being ignored, sidelined, or simply not informed in advance about decisions that would affect it.

On other issues of importance to Turkey, the U.S. policymakers could only deliver so much, despite their diplomatic efforts. They put their weight behind Turkey's successful accession to the Customs Union in December 1995, but they could not get any movement on Turkey's application for full membership of the EU. Additionally, the Clinton administration had little success in getting concessions from the PASOK government of Greece over any of the bilateral Turco-Greek problems, including Cyprus.

Turkey and Europe

In December 1989 the European Council of Ministers received the "Opinion" of the European Commission on Turkey's 1987 application for full membership of the EU. It coincided almost exactly with the fall of the Berlin Wall. The "Opinion" said that accession should not be even considered until 1993; fall-out from events in Eastern Europe must be assessed; the EU must press ahead first with its own integration; and Turkey's economy must continue to develop. In addition, while acknowledging advances, it highlighted the need for Turkey to address the issues of human rights and Cyprus.[5] The "Opinion" was poorly received by the Turkish public, particularly when the Commission declined to tie themselves to any accession timescale whatsoever. Whatever his motives,

Ozal had raised high expectations when he applied for membership. These expectations were unlikely to be met, and disappointment could only damage the pro-West elite. Seen objectively, the Commission's report did not reflect the racial, religious, or dog-in-the-manger attitude portrayed in the Turkish press. It represented genuine concerns about the ability of Turkey to bridge the economic gap, the uncertainties about the impact of its entry, and real uncertainties about the future of the EU. [6]

In 1992 feelings were further exacerbated when the Maastricht Treaty gave the European Parliament (EP) new powers. Accession to the Customs Union was now dependent on their vote, and the broad socialist grouping in the EP began agitating over human rights abuses in Turkey. Allied to the continuing Greek veto on the release of EU funds to Turkey, and the rising violence against Turkish workers in Germany, traditional Turkish sensitivities were inflamed. At the same time, former Eastern-bloc countries began to appear as potential candidates for membership ahead of Turkey, while increasing demands on EU funding Turkey had hoped to benefit from. In this environment, accession to the Customs Union in 1995 could only look like a consolation prize. When the EP grudgingly voted to allow Turkey into the Customs Union on 13 December 1995, any electoral advantage that the DYP government may have garnered from this success had already been dissipated.

Of equal import for the pro-West elite were concerns about the development of a European Security and Defense Identity (ESDI), which threatened to exclude Turkey. The Western European Union (WEU) had always been the body assumed to take this forward and, under the Kohl-Mitterrand axis, the vision was that WEU would be the military arm of the EU. Because only full members of the EU were eligible for WEU membership, Greece could become a member while Turkey, despite recognition of its greater strategic importance, was accorded only associate membership. Many Turks did not understand the WEU, but its rules and stated aspirations fueled an assumption that this was yet another European "club" excluding Turkey. Technically, the WEU had even more binding mutual obligations than NATO. In May 1995 the Defense Committee of the WEU submitted a report to the General Assembly that in diplomatic language drew attention to the difficulties Turkey had in meeting the broader criteria for membership.[7] However, it stated realistically, "Being a security and defence organisation, WEU, while sharing the views of the Council of Europe and the European Union as regards human rights and democracy in Turkey, has an obligation to consider Turkey's role in the region from a slightly different angle."[8] In 1947 only a direct threat from the Soviets had convinced NATO to accept Turkey as a member. A WEU assessment of Turkish interests and potential threats could only provoke a similar debate if Turkey's full membership was discussed. The balance between the perception of Turkey as an asset or a liability might be close.

At the NATO ministerial meeting in June 1996, a political arrangement was at last agreed whereby the European members accepted that under certain circumstances the WEU could be drawn into the NATO Combined Joint Task Force (CJTF) concept. This made Turkey's associate membership of the WEU easier to accept.

Turkey's Relations with the East

Turkey and Russia

In May 1992 Turkey and Russia concluded a treaty on bilateral relations that was heralded as the beginning of a new era in relations between the two states. Agreement had been reached on the outline for a settlement in Nagorno-Karabakh, and it was said that Russia acknowledged Turkey's legitimate interest in the Trans-Caucasus and Central Asia on the grounds of political, economic, cultural, and religious ties to both areas. The honeymoon did not last long. Given the range of incompatible and conflicting interests across the region, it was improbable that relations could remain long undisturbed. As

Russia regained confidence, it pressed to restore its influence in the former Tsarist and Soviet areas of control. The dramatic energy potential of Azerbaijan, Turkmenistan, and Kazakhstan made the stakes very high. At an early stage Russia began to use the CIS to pursue "joint defense of the external borders of the CIS." Under these arrangements there would be coordinated air defense, joint control of border guards, and where appropriate, training and troop basing agreements.

Initially Russia had been concerned about the threat of Islamic fundamentalism in Central Asia. Given the Muslim nature of the republics, the Russians saw Turkish penetration as less threatening than Iranian. By 1993 this sanguine Russian approach was being dispelled. In September, Yeltsin wrote to Demirel expressing anxiety about growing Turkish influence, and making guarded reference to a likely Russian response. By sending this letter "Yeltsin sent a shock wave through Turkey. . . . He reportedly declared that force ceilings established by the CFE treaty for the North Caucasus districts were falling short of responding to Russia's needs, adding that they faced the risk of non-implementation."[9] Gradually, both the Russians and the United States saw the limitations on Turkey carving a dominant position in the area, and also the limitations of Iranian religious influence. In addition, the nature of the Turkic republics militated against Turkish influence. Only in Azerbaijan was the language really similar, and elsewhere history had weakened the cement of ethnic ties. Leaders of the republics soon began to play down the leading role of Turkey, and sought to enhance their own position as independent regional players. Russia was recognized as a far more effective "ally" than Turkey against China or Iran, and as a far greater "threat" or "influence" than anyone. Their major transport links still followed routes laid down under the Soviets. Their armed forces remained almost fully equipped with Russian weaponry, and therefore spares and ammunition would continue to have to come from Russia. In addition, all the senior officers had been in the Red Army and remained very heavily influenced by their military upbringing. Lastly, but by no means of least

97

significance, the republics all had large Russian minorities, which Russia had already declared it had a duty to protect.[10] Despite further Turkish summits held in Istanbul in October 1994, and in Bishkek in August 1995, the Russians, by 1996, had reasserted themselves, de facto, as the dominant influence in Central Asia.

In the Trans-Caucasus the rivalry was more pronounced. Here, Russia, Turkey, and Iran had contiguous frontiers, and a long history of competition and conflict, and all three saw it as an area of the greatest strategic importance. Once again the reality was that Russia held the strongest cards. Turkey traditionally had good relations with Georgia but was forced to watch as Russia used the Abkhazian and South Ossetian revolts as a cover to force a troop-basing agreement on President Shevednadze. In Armenia the Russians took advantage of the Nagorno-Karabakh issue and traditional pro-Russian, anti-Turkish attitudes to conclude a similar agreement. By 1995 Turkey once again faced Russian troops across its northeast borders.

The situation in Azerbaijan was more complicated. Despite Turkish suspicions that the Russians had engineered the removal of the pro-Turkish President Elchibey in 1993, President Aliev proved to be extremely robust in refusing to accept Russian troops back on Azeri soil. His position was weakened by the fact that realization of Azeri oil potential, and resolution of the Nagorno-Karabakh problem, were both dependent on Russia. Turkey's potential to influence events was critically weakened by lack of a common border with Azerbaijan.

The Geopolitics of Oil

Almost all assessments support the contention that oil will continue to be the motor of the world's economy until well into the next century, and that gas will be an equally significant energy source. The republics of the former Soviet Union, including Russia itself, possess enormous reserves of both. The oil reserves under the Caspian Sea and in the Central

Asian republics of Kazakhstan, Turkmenistan, and Uzbekistan are estimated at 25 billion barrels, similar to those in Kuwait, and bigger than Alaska and the North Sea combined. Control over these energy resources, and the export routes out of the Eurasian hinterland began to be seen as central issues of post-Cold War politics. The Western interest in these regions became increasingly strong as the potential became known, investment increased, and Russia aspired to a leading regional role again. Access to Caspian and Central Asian oil would keep world oil prices down, reduce dependency on Middle East oil, and boost the prosperity of the new republics and also that of countries who could offer transit routes. It was assessed that Azerbaijan could generate $2 billion a year in oil revenue, while Georgia could expect $500 million annually from transit rights. Independent and self-sufficient states, bolstered by oil revenues, would deny Russia the chance to establish a de facto sphere of influence in these regions.[11] No one had a greater direct stake in development on these lines than Turkey, who had few indigenous energy resources and rising energy demands.[12]

Geography was against both the West and Turkey in setting the rules of the game. At an early stage Russia identified the leverage it could exert. The Trans-Caucasus was the gateway to the West for Central Asia; therefore, by controlling Georgia and Armenia it had important conrol over energy exports. In the early confusion of the Russian Federation, the Russian military had taken almost independent action to re-establish their hold in Georgia and Armenia. The Russian intervention in Chechenya in December 1994 was partly to ensure control of the Baku-Tikhoretsk pipeline and to seize the Grozny oil refinery with its processing capacity of 12 million tons a year. Russia waited for the Azeris to realize that no oil deal can be done in the face of their opposition or without giving it a larger stake in the $6 billion oil deal between Azerbaijan and an international consortium.

On a blank map, the most advantageous pipeline routes for Turkey would be from Azerbaijan, through Armenia, and south through Turkey to the Mediterranean port of Ceyhan, and from Central Asia, into Iran, and across to Ceyhan. Unfortunately, it could not benefit from either of these. Russian control and its own embargo on Armenia, thwarted the first route. The U.S. policy of containing Iran counted out the second. The oil-producing states would have supported these routes, but they swiftly recognized the realities of their geography. Russian plans saw Azerbaijani oil coming north to Novorossiysk, or to the Georgian port of Sopsa, and then out through the Bosphorus; and Central Asian oil simply going north to Russia and then west. They made some reference to a Sopsa-Ceyhan link, but in May 1996 Turkey withdrew its offer to rehabilitate the pipelines to Sopsa and appeared to have acknowledged the difficulties of getting the Ceyhan link accepted.[13]

Turkey was not in a position to dictate terms, and it held no strong cards to use as leverage against the hard facts of its geographic position. All it could do was object, on safety and environmental grounds, to increased use of the Bosphorus by oil tankers. In reality, assuming there is a pipeline out of Russia, the Black Sea countries, including Turkey, could probably absorb the majority of the oil in domestic consumption, with minimal increase in traffic through the Straits.

While this was going on, Iran also began to flex its economic muscle in the area. Iran had increasingly recognized the minimal impact that its Shiite brand of Islam had had in Central Asia and the penalties of provoking Russia, while still embargoed by the United States.[14] In the face of a critical domestic economic situation, Iran's moderates saw greater advantage in seeking to get economic benefits out of its common border with Turkmenistan and its Caspian links with Kazakhstan. While Turkey was forced to put its faith in ethnic and linguistic ties, Iran could focus on a more pragmatic policy that concentrated on developing trade and infrastructure links. In May 1996 Iran opened a $216 million rail-link across the Turkmen border, which re-opened transport ties from the Gulf into the Russian hinterland, and on to Southeast Asia. Although

Turkey would benefit from a link that dramatically cut transport distances to countries as far away as China, the significance lay in establishing a corridor from Central Asia to the Iranian port of Bandar Abbas. In addition, although Iran had been excluded from the Azeri deal, it had secured an oil swap agreement with the giant U.S.-Kazakh Tenghiz project, giving these landlocked oilfields access to world markets without going through Russia. At the same time it also succeeded in obtaining a 10 percent share in a $4 billion project to develop the Shakh-Deniz oilfield in the Caspian.[15]

Turkey and the Middle East

Turkey had enhanced its Middle East credentials after it broke off full diplomatic relations with Israel in the wake of Israel's 1982 invasion of Lebanon. However, as key players in the Arab world re-engaged with Israel in the 1990s, so Turkey renewed its relationship. On the one hand this gave it leverage against Iran and Syria, while on the other it offered support for U.S. policy in the region and gave Turkey a chance for fuller involvement. While the Middle East Peace Process was in full swing this policy brought advantages, to the extent that Egypt began to fear Turkey might usurp its leadership role in the region. As the Peace Process faltered in early 1996, Turkish support for Israel began to become a liability again, and it was seen and portrayed as anti-Arab. The coincidence of Demirel's visit to Tel Aviv and the signing of a new Turco-Israeli military accord, almost at the same time as Israel's Operation *Grapes of Wrath* in Southern Lebanon, could not have been more poorly timed. The military and the secular parties saw the arrangement in bald political and security terms, but Refah, whose political rhetoric included rabid anti-Semitism, was opposed to a Middle East policy whose cornerstone was alliance with the only non-Muslim country in the region. In Turkish political terms this attitude was not as significant as it appeared. The majority of Turks were contemptuous of the Arabs and still bore memories of the "betrayal" of the First World War. They did not feel they owed the Arab world anything. Security issues were much more important than religious brotherhood. Syrian support for the PKK and Arab League support for the Syrian and Iraqi stance on water rights appeared to show Turkey where its true friends lay. Despite this stance, Turkey continued to argue for the maintenance of Iraq as a unitary state in order to arrest any moves toward establishing a de facto Kurdish state in the region.

Conclusion

Turkey does not share a single border with a friendly country. Allied to its self-denying ordinance over unilateral action and its economic limitations, this severely limits its scope for maneuver. None of the major players in the Balkans, Trans-Caucasus, Middle East or Central Asia has any interest in advancing Turkey's ambitions to play a more significant regional role, and most have a vested interest in thwarting it. Turkey's friends and allies can do little to advance its position, and the state of Turkish politics in 1995/96 undermined its pretentions to be a role model for the new Turkic republics. Antagonism with Greece complicates its relations with the organizations it most desires to join. Potential clashes with its southern neighbors force many in the West to question whether Turkey brings more liabilities than assets to the security equation. Turkey's anomalous situation, and its developing sense of isolation, are compounded by the enthusiasm with which the West seems to seize on both Samuel Huntington's article "Clash of Civilisations?"[16] and the NATO Secretary General's speech of 1995 putting forward Islam as a new threat in the post-Cold War era. With its Janus face, Turkey looks both East and West and finds little real comfort in either direction.

Notes

1. Taken from the title of Ian O. Lesser's paper, *Bridge or Barrier? Turkey and the West after the Cold War,* in, *Turkey's New Geopolitics.*

2. Taken from a lecture at St. Antony's College, Oxford, by Professor Gun Kut of Bogazici University, Istanbul, 27 April 1996.

3. Owing to Greek lobbying, the United States delayed releasing three frigates for which Turkey had paid $130 million, or to complete an order for 10 Cobra helicopters.

4. Interview with Professor Hasan Koni, Head of the Ataturk Institute, Ankara, 7 December 1995.

5. Micheal Cendrowicz, "The European Community and Turkey; Looking Backwards, Looking Forward," in *Turkish Foreign Policy: New Prospects,* ed. Clement H. Dodd (Wistow: Eothen Press, 1992), 17.

6. The U.N. Development Program measures three elements—life expectancy at birth, adult literacy rate, and GNP per capita—to produce a composite "Human Development Index" (HDI) ranking. In 1985 Turkey was ranked 110 out of 130. Paul Kennedy, *Preparing for the 21st Century* (London: Harper Collins, 1993), 351.

7. Assembly of Western European Union, Defense Committee, *The Eastern Mediterranean, Document 1465,* 24 May 1995.

8. Ibid., 9.

9. Duygu Sezer, *Turkey's Political and Security Interests and Policies in the New Geostrategic Environment of the Expanded Middle East* (Washington, DC: The Henry L. Stimson Center, 1994), 8.

10. In Kazakhstan this Russian minority is 38 percent of the population, and concentrated in the Northwest, close to the Russian border and among the major oil and gas fields.

11. The Heritage Foundation, Backgrounder, *The New "Great Game:" Oil Politics in the Caucasus and Central Asia,* Washington, 25 January 1996. This paper, largely written for a Republican audience, convincingly spells out the dangers of allowing Russia to re-establish hegemony in these critical oil-producing areas, but is less good at setting out a realistic agenda to reverse their current success.

12. Turkey estimates that it will have to raise its energy production from 70 million to 270 million kilowatt hours by 2010. To reach this capacity Turkey will have to spend $2 billion per year, and even then Turkey's energy sources will still only provide 38 percent of Turkey's requirements. *Turkish Probe,* 26 Apr 1996.

13. *Financial Times,* 14 May 1996.

14. In addition, Iran had been promised technical assistance from Russia for its nuclear power program.

15. *Financial Times*, 14 May 1996.

16. Samuel P. Huntington, "The Clash of Civilizations?" in *Foreign Affairs* (Summer 1993): 22-49.

8.
Facing the Future

It is Turkey's perception that it is an important country, and Turkey *is* an important country. In fashioning the new republic, Ataturk inherited an Ottoman tradition of state power and a security policy based on fear of Russia and alignment with the West. Ataturk turned this alignment with the West into the foundation of all Turkish policy. The "national mission" would be buttressed by any actions that secured the territorial integrity and unity of Turkey. In his slogans "Happy the man who calls himself Turk" and "Peace at home, peace in the World," Ataturk encapsulated a vision of society that could not accept domestic division, but would not pursue external expansionism. This vision was passed for safekeeping to the military and civil service establishment. Consensus on a "national policy" served Turkey well. Faced with important challenges in three eras of dramatic global change, the ability of Turkey's leaders consistently to identify the national interest allowed it to adapt to new circumstances, taking it through new statehood, World War, global superpower confrontation, and the New World Order without any of the disasters that befell other countries.

But in the foundations of the Turkish state, Ataturk created potential divisions in Turkish society. These divisions were not addressed by his successors, and they became institutionalized by the state elites, either with a vested interest in maintaining their position, or unable to see how to alter society without undermining its cohesion. Ataturk made nationalism a defining aspect of the ideology of the state, although Turkey was a multi-ethnic and multicultural society. To a large extent he succeeded in assimilating the many different ethnic groups within the concept of "Turk," but the "cost of fully entering life in the new Republic was the denial of one's ethnicity."[1] To some groups, most particularly the Kurds, ethnic solidarity was stronger than national solidarity. Additionally, in a country where 99 percent of the population were Muslims, Ataturk made secularism another defining part of the state ideology. While the state elites maintained their secular purity through major socioeconomic change, elements of more traditional Turkish society became increasingly unhappy with what they perceived to be an antireligious bias. Democracy led to the undermining of the "right" of the establishment to dictate the social identity of the country, and its external orientation.

Ataturk had laid down a Western-oriented policy, and through the Cold War necessity marched in step with inclination, overcoming the periods of frustration and ambivalence. The foreign policy objectives of all Turkish governments and all political parties remained broadly similar, and while the depth and intensity of Turkey's association with the West may have been questioned, the fact of it was not. This alignment was heavily subsidized by the West. However, the strong aspiration to be part of the West was not matched by the necessary political, economic and social advances. The economy remained autarkic and nationalist, and these endemic structural problems in the economy increasingly hampered Turkey's integration into the Western economy and stunted the development of a recogniZable middle class. Poor economic development meant poor social development and, consequently, weak political development. All of this contributed to the continuing dominance of the state over civil society, exemplified by the continuity of security policy through 54 governments in 73 years[2] and the "paternalistic" interventions of the military.

The Ozal period highlighted the dilemma. On one side were the few pluralists who saw that Turkey would not be accepted by the West on sentiment alone, and that genuine alignment would come only with modernization and full democracy. On the other side were both the establishment, who feared that pluralism could actually undermine the alignment with the West and might threaten Turkey's territorial integrity and national unity, and the Islamists, who openly challenged this orientation. Even where there was substantial economic advance it provoked division. In the 1980s capitalism, privatization, and the dismantling of statism made Turkey a national "winner" but created many individual "losers." Many objected to the corruption and ostentation this economic advance spawned, and in a democracy, this had important electoral implications. In the 1990s this was increasingly successfully exploited by Refah.

The end of the Cold War was the end of easy consensus. The lifting of a sense of common threat binding Turkey and the West revealed both the domestic and international divisions. Ataturk had set a "national mission" but this was by no means the natural orientation of the country. Under new international pressures and the lack of encouragement, the concept of security policy as a "national policy" was increasingly challenged, or at least questioned. The 1995 and 1996 political maneuverings revealed Turkey's continuing search for a sense of unity and common culture. The Turkish political landscape was now dominated by three competing currents: Kurdish nationalism, Islamism, and Kemalist nationalism. This division had its roots in the inability of Turkey to develop a genuinely pluralistic society that could accommodate differing interpretations of Turkey's destiny. Kurdish nationalists claimed the problem lay in the state's rigid interpretation of Turkish nationalism; Islamists saw the root of the problem in Ataturk's reforms, which deliberately aimed at denying Turkey's Islamic identity. Kemalists saw the crisis as stemming from foreign forces seeking to divide Turkey, and from the antisecular and antinational policies of the first two groups.[3]

Because the internal and external policies of Turkey had always been so closely interlinked, these competing visions of Turkish society inevitably threatened the consensus on foreign policy. Although Turkey acceded to the Customs Union in 1995, remained an active member of NATO, and frequently rededicated itself to the goal of full EU membership, a more active public ambivalence to its relationship with the West began to display itself.[4] This was played on by the increasingly liberalized and vocal media. There was worrying evidence of disillusionment with the West among the establishment, both in the state bureaucracies and in the parties formerly most pro-West, which coincided with the outright rejection professed by the increasingly politically significant Islamists. As traced in this paper, whatever other aspects of Kemalism had been eroded, the state elites had maintained Ataturk's Western orientation whatever the political hue of the government, and whatever the temperature of public opinion. In the main, Turkish foreign policy had always displayed caution, and regard for the good opinion of the international community. Only over Cyprus had they sidelined the principles of Kemalist foreign policy and backed unilateral, aggressive action. From the end of the Cold War, observers noted that not only was there a growing division between state and electorate over the direction of Turkish foreign policy, but even within the state this consistent pro-West foreign policy line was being questioned. A 1995 book on foreign affairs opened with the words:

> The imperialist Western powers, and the rich Christian countries, have always united against the threat from the East, the Eastern peoples, the Ottoman Empire, and the Turks. . . . Turkey is a country that has to live together with the Middle Eastern countries, however much it integrates with Western countries and Europe. In short it cannot be detached from the Middle East.

The significance was that this came not from Islamist, nationalist, or Marxist writings but from a book published by TGS, the organization that was such a bulwark of Ataturk's drive for acceptance by the West.[5] There was evidence that the establishment might be losing the authority, and now the will, to continue imposing the Kemalist line.

Much of this new ambivalence stemmed from external reactions to the intractable Kurdish problem, thereby exacerbating the strong Turkish "Sevres Syndrome." Turks saw the Kurdish issue as a zero-sum game in which anyone with legitimate concerns about human rights abuses was automatically assumed to support a separate Kurdish state. On television in 1995, General Evren, the former president, said "The Western powers have never given up their ambitions . . . the young generations will see that the great powers will take the (Kurdish) Southeast away from us."[6] In the West, the idea that senior military and political figures in Turkey could still believe that there was a conspiracy to dismember their country was greeted with incredulity. However, although it was difficult to discern any advantage the West could gain from weakening Turkey, it was still a sincerely held Turkish opinion, found at all levels of society. Such suspicions were fed by a traditional belief that, despite all its efforts, the West was antipathetic to Turkey, or simply self-serving.

In the West there was agreement that Turkey was a significant regional player and that many issues concerning the West had a strong Turkish dimension. However, assessments on its future varied. The spectrum of opinion ranged from Turkey as a secular, democratic, industrialized member of the West, to Turkey as an Islamized neutralist state, to Turkey riven by internal violence or involved in regional conflict, most worryingly against Greece. What the West was less certain about was how significantly to reinforce Ataturk's original instinct for alignment with the advanced nations. Despite the West's best intentions the options for assistance were limited or constrained by geopolitical realities. Even without these constraints, the inability, or refusal, of Turkey to adjust its domestic structures to the requirements of a genuine pluralistic society, made it difficult to accept it as an equal.

In Turkey, this attitude, allied to public frustration at the inability of Turkey to achieve some of its maximalist ambitions, contributed to an exasperating lack of mutual understanding and an inevitable weakening of sympathy for the West. This was exploited by Islamists and nationalists, thereby undermining the position of the pro-West elite, who again were portrayed as allowing Turkey to be humiliated by the West. These trends threatened to destroy the cohesion of the elite, whose control of state power has been so critical in ensuring that Turkey has pursued such a consistently minimalist foreign policy, despite external provocation and periodic political instability. This trend was not helped by the inability of the center-right political parties (ANAP and DYP) to put aside personal animosities in the face of an Islamist challenge to the state. The cynicism, corruption, and short-termism of the political maneuverings after the 1995 elections were damaging to all the secular parties. It also undermined its own, and the West's, hopes that Turkey would provide the example of a Muslim, secular, and democratic society to other states in the region.

When all this has been said, there was an inertia built into alignment with the West that even Refah recognized, as its early government policy pronouncements made clear. However unsatisfactory it felt the current relationship with the West to be, there was simply no market that could replace Europe and the United States, or which offered such potential. The Turkish people's acceptance of Ataturk's "national mission" lay not only in the attachment to his memory and legacy, but also in the obvious results of modern development. When Turks looked at other countries in the region only Israel impressed them. Additionally there was no substitute for the security that membership of NATO offered, particularly while the future of Russia remained uncertain. The NATO-WEU accord on security arrangements lessened Turkey's concerns over an European security identity that excluded its and Turkey's relationship with the West would also be easier if the EU were now also to develop on the principle of broader, rather than deeper, integration. Domestically there was a vibrant private sector economy, and there was general public support for secularism, or a secularism that more openly acknowledged the Muslim nature of society. Turkey was not

110

directly threatened, its regional strength and influence was acknowledged, if not welcomed, and although its early aspirations in the Turkic world had been frustrated, Turkey could afford to settle down for the long haul.

However, the coming to power of a Refah-dominated coalition, even in an alliance with the secular DYP, understandably caused major concerns among Turkey's allies. The United States had been particularly scarred over Iran, and all the West had developed a suspicion and fear of Islamic fundamentalism, deepened by events in Algeria. Western reaction to an Erbakan government was like that of the Turkish military: wait and see. At this stage Refah had little option but to be responsible. They had broken the taboos of 73 years of secularism, the military had not intervened, the stock market and currency had not collapsed, and there had been a guarded response from abroad. However, any chance of Refah achieving anything radical depended on a future, more emphatic election success, and that depended on convincing critics and sceptics, at home and abroad, that they were a serious, responsible, democratic party of government. They could not yet achieve the two-thirds majority in the GNA required to change the constitution nor, against the military bloc, would they gain control of the NSC.

While the establishment, and particularly the armed forces, still adhered to secularism and Kemalist foreign policy principles, they limited the ability of politicians or public to drive Turkey into adventurism, or radically to alter Turkey's foreign policy orientation. However, the move of Islamists into mainstream Turkish politics called into question many former assumptions, and a Turkish government, even a coalition government, that was not psychologically aligned with the West complicated Western security calculations in the region. Domestically, even some secularists thought the Refah success may prove to have a healthy dimension. Refah would now have to match their actions to their words. They would have to operate within the economic and geo-political limitations of Turkey. They would have to make the compromises and

111

concessions that all governments have to make. They may genuinely push Turkey closer to being a more pluralist society, or act as the catalyst that convinced the establishment that reform was inevitable and that it was better to lead it than to oppose it, or simply follow it. Therefore this first experiment in Islamist-dominated government represented an important development, yet one that was vulnerable, uneasy, watched by a dubious military, and likely to splinter easily.

Erbakan initially adopted many of the existing policy stances on security issues, accepting a division of responsibility that left the security portfolios with the DYP. Refah needed U.S. support over many issues, and their social program was unattainable without the continuing assistance of the IMF and World Bank. The rhetoric over Customs Union, the European Union, and NATO may be new, but Islamist pronouncements would probably be accompanied by secularists being despatched to put Western minds at rest, and delegations sent to the military to reassure them that Kemalist principles were not being threatened. In a more encouraging move, during his visit to Southeast Asia in August 1996, Erbakan echoed Gokalp's enthusiasm for Japan when he, too, portrayed that country as a modern role model for Turkey. Even closer to home was his endorsement of Malaysia as a Muslim country that was also a confident player in the global economy.

The continuing firm, if reluctant support for the U.S. policy of dual-containment in the region was inevitably going to come under pressure. Turkish policy seemed likely to move closer to other Muslim countries and further from the Israelis. The early suspension of the Turkish-Israeli military agreement, the enthusiasm for renewed trade with Iraq, and the multibillion dollar oil deal with Iran were early indications of this new shift in orientation. However, Erbakan exerted significant party discipline to ensure that a revised format for Operation *Provide Comfort* was voted for by Refah deputies in the GNA. In addition, Erbakan was a Turk and a nationalist. It was fair to assume that if there was no reciprocal movement on such issues as support for the PKK and water rights, his new accommodation with Muslim neighbours could be reversed or diluted.

Over Cyprus and Aegean issues the Refah-DYP coalition would be more hardline and nationalist than ANAP, seeking political capital out of a vigorous and public defense of Turkish interests.[78] Ciller's credentials had already been established during the Kardak confrontation of early 1996, and the coalition was united in a vigorous response to renewed Greek agitation in Cyprus in August 1996. Against strong Turkish military and public concern Refah might in time support the softening of the cultural impositions in Kurdish areas, but they dared not yet hint at anything that might imply, or encourage, autonomy or separatism.

What the long-term implications of this new political landscape will be for the West depends on how sure the establishment's hand remains on the levers of state power. In Turkish society, a Western orientation is still broadly supported by the 79 percent of the electorate who did not vote for Refah in 1995. But, perversely, the establishment simultaneously advocate, pursue, yet undermine this orientation. Until major adjustments are made in the economy, a number of issues— the constitutional position on human rights, the role of the security forces in society, the Kurdish problem, the issue of democratic pluralism in the broadest sense, the relationship with the West—can never develop fully. Refah have certainly further complicated the situation. Maybe this is inevitable, given the nature of Turkey. Currently it is difficult to be optimistic about developments in Turkey, given the lack of political power or authority in civil society, and the lack of vision in the state.

Refah may push too forcefully against the constraints in Turkish politics and provoke a response by the military. If they do not provoke the military directly, their Islamic conservatism may yet push the Alewites into violent opposition, giving the Army a reason to intervene on a "law and order" basis. In the pursuit of domestic consensus the coalition may run against

113

traditional cautious Turkish policy, seeking to externalize their internal problems by provoking confrontation with Greece or Syria. Conversely Greece, Syria, or another neighbor may seek to take advantage of Turkey's internal problems thereby provoking a conflict. All these scenarios would put the relationship between Turkey and the West into an impossibly difficult situation and give enormous encouragement both to Turkey's enemies and all those who would wish to detach Turkey from the West.

The best outcome for the West would be that the pragmatists in Refah recognize the advantages of alignment with the West, while accepting the current, broad limitations on their actions. In such a case political "froth" will cover the fact that little has changed. However things do *need* to change. Erbakan's public espousal of such countries as Japan and Malaysia give some hope that even the Islamists recognize that Turkey is *sui generis* and must find a workable compromise between its material ambitions, its legitimate security concerns, and its Muslim identity. "Peace in the World" is very much in Turkey's interests, and the West must do all it can to shape circumstances to help it. "Peace at Home" lies more directly in Turkey's own hands.

Ultimately there is a need for Turkey to help itself, thereby allowing the West to help Turkey. There is the most important mutual interest in this. The West cannot afford to "lose" such a valuable country, in such an important region, at such a critical period. A proud, important country like Turkey, with enormous potential, must not be allowed or encouraged to "reject" the West, thereby turning from its legitimate and historical goal of "achieving the level of contemporary civilization." The old joke that "the situation is critical, but it is not serious" used to reflect an underlying stability in Turkey, and the self-adjusting nature of the relationship between state and society. The danger is that in this new environment the situation in Turkey becomes both critical *and* serious.

114

NOTES

1. Quoted in Soli Ozel, "Of Not Being a Lone Wolf: Geography, Domestic Plays, and Turkish Foreign Policy in the Middle East," in *Powder Keg in the Middle East: The Struggle for Gulf Security*, eds., Geoffrey Kemp and Janice Gross Stein (London: Lanham, Rowman and Littlefield, 1995), 182.

2. Given that the CHP had a monopoly of power from 1923 to 1946, and continued in power until 1950, there have now been 53 governments in 47 years.

3. M. Hakan Yavaz, "Turkey's "Imagined Enemies": Kurds and Islamists," in *The World Today* 52, no. 4 (April 1996): 99.

4. In a 1995 independent poll, 50 percent of Turks said they felt their place was in Europe, while the rest were equally divided between the "Islamic" and "Turkic" worlds. To the question "Which nations are the best friends of Turkey?" 30 percent now said that "Turkey has no friends", while 25 percent saw the United States as their greatest enemy, and 23 percent gave Greece this accolade. Japan now featured as the most favoured nation, replacing the 1960s preference for Germany. In the 1995 elections Refah and the DSP, parties with the strongest anti-West and anti-European credentials, did well in the elections. Although diametrically opposed on social and religious policies, their combined vote represented 37 percent of the electorate (Sahin Alpay, in *The Independent*, 22 May 1996, 24.

5. Ibid.

6. Ibid.

7. Interview with Sami Kohen, foreign affairs editor of *Milliyet*, Istanbul, 5 July 1996.

8. Interview with Soli Ozel, Bogazici University, Istanbul, 12 July 1996.

About the Author

Lieutenant Colonel S. V. Mayall is currently Commanding Officer of the Queen's Dragoon Guards of the British Army. He is a veteran of the Persian Gulf War and has served as Military Assistant to the Deputy Supreme Allied Commander, Europe.   Lieutenant Colonel Mayall received an M.A. from Oxford and attended the Army Staff College. From 1995-1996, he was a Defence Fellow of St. Antony's College, Oxford.